SUZANNE GOLDEN PRESENTS

PRESENTS

Interviews with 36 Artists Who Innovate with Beads

LARK JEWELRY
& BEADING

Editor
Nathalie Mornu

Production Editor
Julie Hale

Art Director
Kathleen Holmes

Editorial Assistants
Dawn Dillingham
Hannah Doyle

Designer
Carol Morse Barnao

Cover Designer
Laura Palese

**Front cover,
clockwise from top left**

Christine Marie Noguere,
*Alma Venus (Jewelry for
Giants, No. 1)*, 2006

Isabell Schaupp,
Four Ears (Brooch), 2010

Teresa Sullivan,
If He Hollers, 2007

Lynne Sausele,
Summer Way, 2011

Suzanne Golden, *Desert
Bloom Bracelet*, 2010

Marina Dempster, *Mutable—
adj. 1. Subject to change
or alteration. 2. Prone to
frequent change; inconsistent;
fickle. 3. Capable of change
or of being changed.*, 2007

Spine

Jan Huling, *Koko Monkey*, 2011

Back cover, left to right

Christy Puetz, *Nigel*, 2009

Helena Markonsalo,
My Little Armour, 2003

Opposite

Ceaser Nhlenhe Mkhize and
Mildred Thafa Dlamini,
Sobohla Manyosi, 2009

I would like to dedicate this book to the memory of my parents, Rebecca and Mortimer Golden, and my sister, Barbara; to my nephew, Adam, for his constant encouragement; to my wonderful friends; and to the beading community for their acknowledgment and continued support of my work.

—Suzanne Golden

LARK CRAFTS

An Imprint of Sterling Publishing
387 Park Avenue South
New York, NY 10016

Text © 2013, Lark Crafts, an Imprint of Sterling Publishing Co., Inc.

ISBN 978-1-4547-0410-2

Library of Congress Cataloging-in-Publication Data

Suzanne Golden presents interviews with 36 artists who innovate with beads. -- First edition.
    pages cm. -- (Lark jewelry & beading spotlight on beading)
  Includes index.
  ISBN 978-1-4547-0410-2 (pbk.)
  1. Beadwork. 2. Beadworkers--Interviews. I. Golden, Suzanne. II. Title.
  TT860.S89 2013
  745.594'2--dc23

2012037308

Distributed in Canada by Sterling Publishing
c/o Canadian Manda Group, 165 Dufferin Street
Toronto, Ontario, Canada M6K 3H6
Distributed in the United Kingdom by GMC Distribution Services
Castle Place, 166 High Street, Lewes, East Sussex, England BN7 1XU
Distributed in Australia by Capricorn Link (Australia) Pty. Ltd.
P.O. Box 704, Windsor, NSW 2756, Australia

For information about custom editions, special sales, and premium and corporate purchases, please contact Sterling Special Sales at 800-805-5489 or specialsales@sterlingpublishing.com.

Email academic@larkbooks.com for information about desk and examination copies.
The complete policy can be found at larkcrafts.com.

Manufactured in China

2 4 6 8 10 9 7 5 3 1

larkcrafts.com

contents

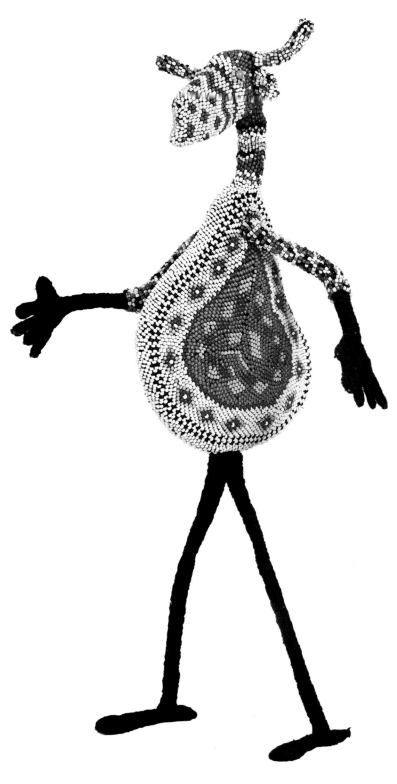

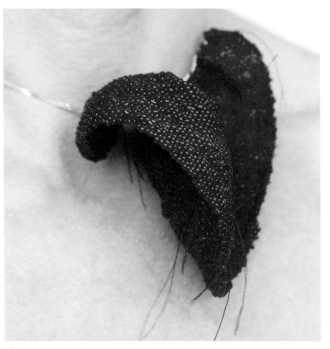

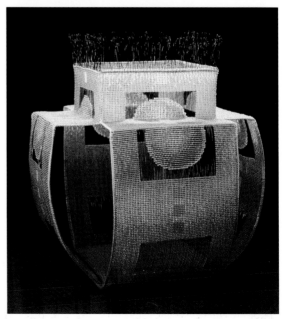

introduction

you can do so much with beads when you regard them as an art form.

For this volume, I asked 36 outstanding artists about how they use beads. The resulting interview text is accompanied by images of their work and brief autobiographical information. When I was asked to curate this book, I felt very flattered. I've been beading for about two decades and have a definite opinion and sense of style. It was nice that Lark Jewelry & Beading wanted to know what I have to say about beading. I decided I wanted this volume to show that beads can be so much more than just a necklace or a pair of earrings. In these pages, you'll see beads used to create art, the kind of sculptural work or high-end jewelry that would be in a gallery. Artwork and jewelry have value not just because of the materials used to make them, but because of the work involved. In this book, the medium simply happens to be beads.

The selection of beads has expanded, and we have so many different bead stitches from which to choose. But it's what we do with the techniques that makes our work unique. There are no rules in beading. I realized one day that the look I wanted my finished pieces to have could only be achieved by using acrylic or plastic beads, which provided a more intense color palette. I'm now one of the few beaders to use plastic beads. I'm delighted to feel secure enough in my taste to use whatever shades I want and then embellish to my heart's content. I've seen my own style of beading change, and I hope it's still evolving.

While creating the list of beaders to include in the book, I sought to include the greatest variety possible, but especially artists who impressed with their workmanship. If I saw new work and my reaction was, "Why didn't I think of that?" or, "That's impressive and I would never be able to do it," it's a fair bet I invited that artist to participate. I wanted to share this bounty and diversity with you, challenge you, open your eyes, give you a different way of looking at beading, make you exclaim "wow!" and inspire you.

The imagery here spans a wide range. It includes the incredible, large-scale work of Nick Cave, Felieke van der Leest's humorous pieces, delicate, graceful jewelry by Jina Lee, and totally charming figures made by Uliana Volkhovskaya. I think the book has a wonderful diversity of beadwork to satisfy everyone.

If not for the Internet, I don't know how I would have found all the information I did. Looking up various art and jewelry websites and those of galleries from all over the world opened up a whole new art world and helped me find beadwork and artists I would never otherwise have known about. One connection led to another, and another, and another.

I loved all aspects of working on this book—researching, discovering the wonderful work being done with beads, whittling down my list to 36 artists, selecting their images, and writing about them. The book you hold in your hands represents the kind of work I would exhibit if I owned an art gallery. I hope you love it.

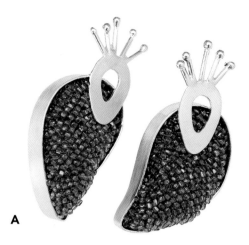

A

ulli kaiser

I was born in Austria and studied textile art and art education, with an emphasis on painting, at the Universität für Musik und darstellende Kunst "Mozarteum" Salzburg, gaining the degree *Magister Artium* (Masters in Arts) with honors. After years in Hong Kong, where I taught art and was involved in bookbinding, Asian jewelry, and textile techniques, I moved to England in 1989. I continued learning new crafts like upholstery, felting, mosaics, beading, and jewelry making. I design and work from my home in Guildford, Surrey, where I live with my three children.

www.ullikaiser.co.uk

B

A *Earrings*, 2012
3 x 2 x 1 cm
Vintage glass seed beads, sterling silver; crocheted, hand fabricated
Photo by Christian Kaiser

B *Necklace*, 2009
47 x 4 x 3 cm
Vintage and contemporary glass seed beads, sterling silver; crocheted, peyote stitch, hand fabricated
Photo by Christian Kaiser

C *Rings*, 2011
4 x 3 x 2 cm
Vintage and contemporary glass seed beads, sterling silver; crocheted, hand fabricated
Photo by Christian Kaiser

C

"Bead crochet takes a great deal of time, and that doesn't get acknowledged. Adding silver elements shifts the perception from beadwork to fine jewelry, increasing the value of the technique."

D

E

D *Rings*, 2011
4 x 2 x 2 cm
Glass seed beads, antique metal beads, blue goldstone, sterling silver; crocheted, hand fabricated
Photo by Christian Kaiser

E Detail of *Necklace*, 2008
49 x 2 x 2 cm
Vintage and contemporary glass seed beads, crystals, felt, cotton, chrysocolla, polymer clay, turquoise, apatite, acrylic, sterling silver, stem coral, pearls; crocheted, peyote stitch, hand fabricated
Photo by Christian Kaiser

WHEN DID YOU BEGIN MAKING JEWELRY?
I started seven years ago with stringing, and subsequently taught myself bead crochet, inspired by the gift of a crocheted pearl necklace as well as the work of Austria's Wiener Werkstatte during the 1920s. For the past five years I've attended silversmithing workshops, and still enjoy learning new techniques that I can incorporate into my jewelry.

YOU WERE CROCHETING BEADS AND SOMEHOW JUMPED INTO INCORPORATING METALSMITHING INTO YOUR WORK. HOW DID YOU MAKE THIS LEAP?
During my studies I was already fascinated by the tension that can be created between different materials and their color combinations. After experimenting with what ways and what kind of materials bead crochet can be used, I found myself stuck in production instead of creating. Initially, I started silversmithing to make clasps and to finish off beaded beads. Nevertheless, after a few workshops with silversmiths—who usually work big, whereas jewelers work fine and small—I quickly found

myself creating small "vessels." The doors then opened wide and I added new shapes and textures, new contrasts and visual interest. Adding silver elements also lifted the beadwork to another level.

PLEASE DESCRIBE YOUR WORKING PROCESS. Everything evolves during the making. It's a process of give and take. I do start with an image in my mind and sometimes on paper, but after choosing the materials, the colors, and the techniques, it evolves, and the creating starts. I try to achieve a balance, a symbiosis between bead crochet and silver, without having one dominate the other, and to form a relationship between the different elements, with stark and prominent contrasts but nevertheless making sure the pieces have a harmonious flow.

WHAT INSPIRES YOUR WORK? I enjoy collecting beads or items I can turn into beads, and I draw inspiration from those materials and their

A

B

C

A *Necklace*, 2011
45 x 3 x 1 cm
Freshwater seed pearls, antique metal beads, vintage and
contemporary glass seed beads, labradorite, crystals, felt,
vintage mink, hematite, sterling silver; crocheted, peyote
stitch, hand fabricated, cast
Photos by Christian Kaiser

B *Necklace*, 2009
48 x 2 x 2 cm
Vintage and contemporary glass seed beads, crystals, felt,
cotton, chrysocolla, polymer clay, turquoise, apatite, acrylic,
sterling silver; crocheted, peyote stitch, hand fabricated
Photo by Christian Kaiser

C *Pendant*, 2010
7 x 5 x 3 cm
Vintage and contemporary glass seed beads, sterling silver;
crocheted, peyote stitch, hand fabricated
Photo by Christian Kaiser

shapes. I also get very
inspired by old botanical
drawings and illustra-
tions of tiny underwater
sea creatures, in par-
ticular the ones by
Ernst Häckel.

**WHAT RESPONSES
DO YOU GET TO THE
JEWELRY?**
"Unique," "exquisite,"
"incredible craftsman-
ship," and that my work
has its own voice and
identity. People tell me
the work reminds them
of the faceted eyes of
insects and the dangly
appendages of under-
water creatures.

**HOW DO YOU CHOOSE
THE BEADS YOU USE?**
I'm always on the look-
out for vintage beads:
in flea markets, when
traveling, on the Inter-
net, in charity shops.
The smaller the beads,
the better. My choice
for any particular piece
depends on the color
and the quantity I have
available.

"Ulli's work is elegant,
refined, soft-spoken.
It invites the viewer
to stop and examine
the finesse of the
workmanship!"
—SUZANNE GOLDEN

stephan hampala

A *Cufflinks,* 2011
Diameter, 1.6 cm; 2 cm tall
Antique glass beads,
wooden spheres, silver
Photo by Bettina Dürrheim

A

I was born in Germany, but grew up in Austria, where I studied history and the theory of theater and the performing arts at the University of Vienna. While researching European costume history, I came across examples of beaded jewelry, which appealed to two of my main interests simultaneously: orna-mentation and textiles. Stimulated by the designs of the Wiener Werkstätte and an interest in ethnic beadwork, I began design-ing my own jewelry using beadwork techniques.

I currently reside in Vienna, where more often than not the urban bustle is quite a welcome change to the calm and steady working rhythm dictated by the beads. Although I sometimes fantasize about being part of a team, I'm continuously captivated by this meticu-lous, deliberate, rather meditative work, which requires concentrated devotion—and in my case necessitates listening to opera: the more passion-ate the better!

B

"Antique beads bring along their own stories— and I love listening."

C

D

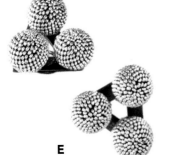

E

B *Necklace*, 2012
Bead diameter, 1.1 cm;
46 cm long
Antique glass and steel beads,
wooden spheres, oxidized silver,
magnetic clasp
Photo by Bettina Dürrheim

C *Necklace*, 2005
Bead diameter, 2.2 cm;
50 cm long
Antique glass beads, wooden
spheres, oxidized silver
Photo by Peter Völker

D *Brooch*, 2005
4 x 4 x 1 cm
Antique glass beads, wooden
spheres, oxidized silver,
steel wire
Photo by Peter Völker

E *Earrings*, 2012
1.8 x 2.1 x 1 cm
Antique metallic glass beads,
wooden spheres, oxidized silver
Photo by Bettina Dürrheim

YOUR JEWELRY LOOKS VERY CONTEMPORARY. YOU STUDIED EUROPEAN COSTUME AND JEWELRY DESIGN. HOW DID THIS INFLUENCE YOUR STYLE? WAS THERE A TIME PERIOD THAT MOST AFFECTED YOU?
Various time periods presumably influence my style in general, mostly subconsciously. I can sometimes trace color combinations or forms to specific eras, but otherwise it has more to do with a basic awareness of texture and composition ingrained by my studies in costume history.

HOW DID YOU BEGIN MAKING JEWELRY/ BEADING?
One frequently comes across beadwork from the nineteenth and early twentieth centuries in Vienna. I've always had a weakness for crafts-manship that requires an adherance to detail and the specific needs of unique materials, and a predilection for hand-crafts that may seem outmoded.

During my studies, I was asked to restore an old piece of jewelry. I had to explore various techniques and simply became engrossed in this work.

HOW DO YOU CHOOSE THE BEADS YOU USE?

What I love most is working with old beads, not only because of their colors but even more so because of their irregular cut. This allows me to select a bead of exactly the size and shape necessary to let patterns develop over tapering spheres without distortion and to accomplish a truly precise structure. It's time-consuming but rewarding.

WHAT TYPES OF RESPONSES DOES YOUR WORK GET?

Most people react immediately and directly to the beauty of the materials, the colors, the work. At one point or another, they ask about the amount of time I devote to creating each individual piece.

There's sometimes still (albeit less and less, thankfully) the disbelief that this is work created by a man. And often the assumption that I must be incredibly patient—I'm not.

I've noticed an increased understanding of the uncompromising nature of the workmanship over the value of the material.

A

A *Necklace*, 2008
Bead diameter, 2.3 cm; 48 cm long
Antique glass beads, wooden
spheres, silver, magnetic clasp
Photo by Peter Völker

B *Earrings*, 2010
2.1 x 2.1 x 1 cm
Antique glass beads, wooden
spheres, oxidized silver
Photo by Peter Völker

C *Brooches*, 2010
Diameter, 1.3 cm; 10 cm long
Antique glass beads, wooden
spheres, silver, steel wire
Photo by Peter Völker

B

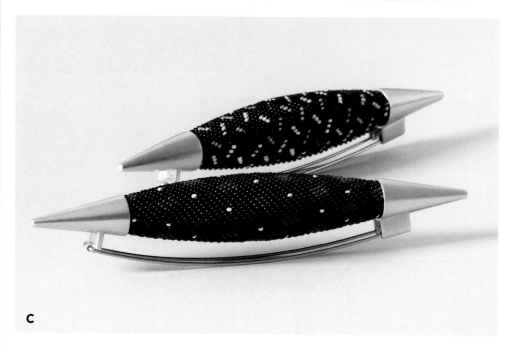

C

12

D *Earrings*, 2005
Diameter, 1.7 cm; 5 cm long
Antique glass beads, wooden
spheres, oxidized silver
Photo by Peter Völker

E *Pendants*, 2008
Diameter, 2.8 cm; 8 cm long
Antique glass beads, wooden
spheres, oxidized silver, silk cord
Photo by Peter Völker

D

E

HOW DO YOU DESIGN PIECES?

I start playfully, trying out color combinations and patterns. As soon as a design surfaces, though, planning sets in and my method becomes very precise. My favorite part is the moment when a tension arises and what was previously unconnected now forms a structure.

WHAT INSPIRES YOU?

The structure of fabrics. The play of color combinations I encounter when I'm out. Fashion.

HAS YOUR WORKING PROCESS EVOLVED OVER TIME?

Aside from the technical ease developed over the years, I've learned to savor the restrictions of the material, plumbing its depths and exploring the limits. The reduced availability of attractive beads, their delicacy, the small dimensions of my jewelry—what are the possibilities of creating patterns on such minute playing fields?

"Less is more with Stephan's jewelry, which makes a very strong statement. Clean lines plus strong, graphic shapes equals eminently wearable."

—SUZANNE GOLDEN

lynne sausele

"I feel connected to the ancient roots of adornment and to jewelry's power to enhance the human spirit."

A graduate of the Boston Museum School and Tufts University, I work as a freelance artist. Over the course of my career, I've been a jewelry designer and a painter. I've found that the two disciplines inspire each other. The designs I create for my pieces are modern and unique, yet they follow some of the most traditional uses of beads. I delight in participating in a practice that's been going on for thousands of years. The seaside town of Gloucester, Massachusetts, is now home for me. I have a beautiful studio in my house and share a gallery space with my husband, Hans Pundt, a collage and assemblage artist.

www.lynnesausele.com

A

A *Provence Necklace/Bracelet*, 2012
107 x 6 x 6 cm
Seed beads, crystals, thread
Photo by Robert Diamante

B *Have Some Fun*, 2012
55 x 1 x 1 cm
Seed beads, wood beads; peyote stitch
Photo by Robert Diamante

C *Play*, 2010
30 x 3 x 3 cm
Handmade beads, seed beads, vintage glass beads, thread; peyote stitch
Courtesy of Mobilia Gallery
Photo by Robert Diamante

C

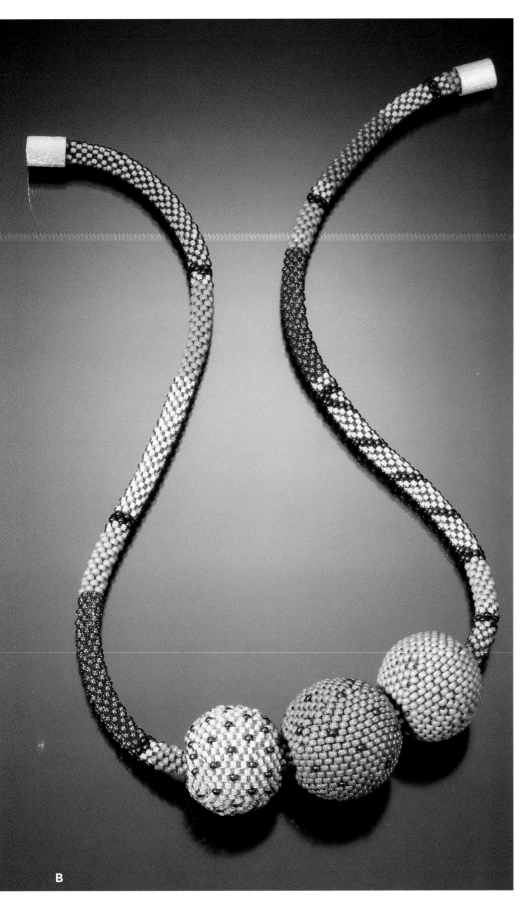

B

TELL US ABOUT YOUR COLOR SENSIBILITY AND PATTERN CHOICES.

Color is my favorite aspect of working with beads. I'm a jewelry designer but also a painter, which has made me sensitive to color. Working with beads allows me to do a great deal of color designing because the hues of beads are so amazing. As for patterns, I prefer a simple approach because I'm more interested in the colorway of a piece.

HOW DO YOU DESIGN?

I usually come up with an idea, then do a quick sketch in a book I keep in my studio so I can refer back to it. I will then take a look at my bead supply and choose the colors that work best with the idea. The process of building the piece comes next. That's when I allow my intuitive sense to take over, because I'll invariably make changes as I go along.

WHEN AND HOW DID YOU BEGIN MAKING JEWELRY?

I made my first pair of earrings for myself, for a trip I took to Hawaii with my sister. I'd been working on some collage-style paintings with gold leaf and decided to make some earrings with the materials I was using. On the trip, many people asked where I got my earrings. I realized right then that I had something new to explore.

HOW DID YOU GET INTO BEADING?

This was a gradual process. I started out making essentially paper jewelry that needed some embellishment, so I used beads as spacers and findings. These pieces ended up in boutiques and museum shops. I created a nice business for myself. I gradually began working more and more with beads because they were so much fun!

B

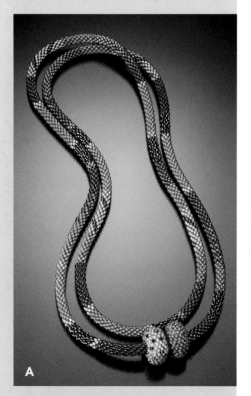

A

C

A *Autumn Spectrum*, 2010
107 x 6 x 6 cm
Seed beads, thread;
peyote stitch
Photo by Robert Diamante

B *Summer Way*, 2011
107 x 6 x 6 cm
Seed beads,
teardrop beads, thread
Courtesy of Mobilia Gallery
Photo by Robert Diamante

C *Summer Necklace*, 2012
48 x 2 x 2 cm
Seed beads, crystals,
freshwater pearls, turquoise;
peyote stitch
Courtesy of Mobilia Gallery
Photo by Robert Diamante

D *Untitled*, 2011
Necklace: 48 x 1 x 1 cm
Earrings: 7 x 2 x 1 cm each
Seed beads, thread, 14-karat
gold wire; peyote stitch
Courtesy of Mobilia Gallery
Photo by Robert Diamante

E *Signs of Spring*, 2010
46 x 2.5 x 2.5 cm
Seed beads, crystals, thread,
labradorite, Picasso stone,
14-karat gold chain
Courtesy of Mobilia Gallery
Photo by Robert Diamante

DO YOU HAVE ANY ADVICE FOR OTHER BEADERS?
Because I feel that color is important to a piece, and I know a lot of people haven't had the opportunity to learn color theory, I recommend getting some tools to help with color design. I see many pieces that are technically amazing but miss the mark in terms of color selection. If I feel stuck in my color choices, I use a paint chart—the kind you can get for free at a paint store. These charts often have extensive groupings of colors. Also, look at what other bead artists are doing. Visit a bead store or flip through bead books. Mimic a colorway that someone else has used. These are all good ways of getting a sense of what colors work well together.

"I like Lynne's work because of her color choices and the texture in her beads. I want to wear her necklaces!"

—SUZANNE GOLDEN

marina dempster

"I use the shoe form to bring attention to the metaphoric paths we fear to take and the literal imprints we leave behind."

My hybrid art practice is a result of my hybrid cultural identity: I was born in Mexico to British and French parents and have lived in Canada since the age of three. I make mixed-media works that blend sculpture, fiber, beading, and painting. Toronto is my home base, and I'm passionate about fostering artistic development in my community. With that goal in mind, I've curated a variety of exhibitions and facilitated hands-on workshops. Photography is another area of interest for me, and my pictures have won various awards over the years.

www.marinadempster.com

A

B

A *Mutable—adj. 1. Subject to
change or alteration. 2. Prone to
frequent change; inconsistent;
fickle. 3. Capable of change or
of being changed.*, 2007
20 x 28 x 23 cm
Donated shoes, *cera de campeche*,
glass seed beads, crystal beads,
silk and cotton threads,
dyed badger hair
Photo by artist

B *Sensational—adj. 1. Of or relating to
sensation or the senses. 2. Suggesting
drama or a stage performance, as in
emotionality or suspense. 3. Particularly
excellent.*, 2008
13 x 18 x 20 cm
Found shoe, *cera de campeche*, galvanized
silver and gold beads, laces,
hand-painted wool
Collection of N. Barry Lyon
Photo by artist

**HOW WOULD YOU
DESCRIBE YOUR WORK?**
I refer to my work as
sculpture, using the
term's secondary defi-
nition as a natural mark
or other impression on
an animal or a plant.
My primary technique
is a contemporary
translation of the pre-
Columbian Huichol
art of transformational
yarn painting. This in-
volves preparing a form
with a skin of beeswax
and pine resin called
cera de campeche,
which is then meticu-
lously embedded with
yarn or beads and
other materials using
the pressure of the
fingertips and impro-
vised tools.

**WHO INTRODUCED
YOU TO BEADING?**
When I was seven or
eight, a girlfriend of my
dad's, who was a gifted
Montessori teacher,
taught me how to use
a small vintage bead
loom. She had a seem-
ingly magical basket of
beads of all kinds that
I loved to rummage
through, and I started
designing bracelets on
graph paper. I've loved
beads ever since. I
was introduced to the
Huichol art of embed-
ding beads in *cera de
campeche* some 10
years ago at a workshop
conducted by Alejandro
Lopez Torres, a Huichol
shaman and artist.

A

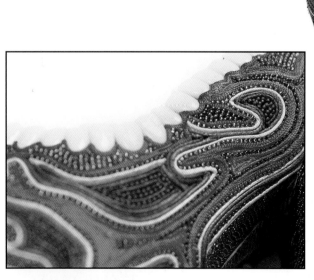

B

WHY DO YOU USE SHOES?
The shoe was a natural
step from other forms
relating to the body that
I used in my previous
work. I view shoes as
extensions of the body,
as feelers or organs of
touch. The shoe as both
a utilitarian object and a
form with endless design
possibilities has the ability to engage the viewer
on multiple levels.

**DO YOU PLAN MUCH
BEFORE YOU BEGIN
WORK, OR DO YOU
DESIGN AS YOU MAKE?**
For the most part, my
designs are improvised
and evolve as they're in
process. At every stage
of the work, whether it
be hunting and gathering
materials or preparing my
form, I make decisions
that connect to the devel-
oping theme or emotion
I want to play with.

A *Horny—adj. 1. Of or resembling
horn—i.e., hard and rough.
2. Feeling or arousing sexual
excitement. 3. Having a horn
or horns.*, 2009
28 x 28 x 23 cm
Found shoe, *cera de campeche*, glass
and metallic seed beads, antique
deer antlers, recycled rabbit fur from
vintage coat
Photos by artist

B *Voracious—adj. 1. Having a very
eager approach to an activity.
2. Having a huge appetite.*, 2008
13 x 18 x 23 cm
Leather shoe, *cera de campeche*,
yarns, glass seed beads, antique
false teeth
Photos by artist

C *Ebullient—adj. 1. Cheerful and
full of energy. 2. Agitated as if
boiling.*, 2008
20 x 12 x 22 cm
Found shoe, *cera de campeche*, glass
and metallic seed beads, Scarlet
Macaw feathers
Photo by artist

C

HOW HAS YOUR WORKING PROCESS EVOLVED OVER TIME?

The way that I use beads has become more refined. With each piece, I use a new material or a familiar one in a different way. Despite being attracted to smaller and smaller beads and to more labor-intensive ways of laying beads, I seem to be making simpler designs.

HOW DO YOU CHOOSE THE BEADS YOU USE?

I often choose beads intuitively, simply because I'm attracted to them. I don't always know where or how they'll end up. The smaller the beads, the better. When I use seed beads, I have more control over the lines and gradations I want to make. I also like to use multiples of found natural objects in my work—items like shells, thorns, or pebbles that have beadlike qualities.

A

A *Defensive—adj. 1. Used or intended to defend or protect. 2. Very anxious to challenge or avoid criticism.*, 2007
13 x 18 x 20 cm
Vintage shoe, *cera de campeche*, glass seed beads, silk thread, gilded thorns, crystals
Photos by artist

B *Immune—adj. 1. Having immunity to infection. 2. Exempt, as from obligation or duty. 3. Protected from danger.*, 2006
15 x 40 x 15 cm
Found shoes, *cera de campeche*, glass seed beads, spiral rope chain, silk threads, recycled rabbit fur, porcupine quills, Scarlet Macaw and flamingo feathers
Photos by artist

B

"I need to add these
shoes to my own shoe
collection…but only to
be admired, though if I
could wear them,
I would!"

—SUZANNE GOLDEN

bcxsy

Established in 2007, BCXSY is a cooperative between Israeli designer Boaz Cohen and Japanese artist Sayaka Yamamoto. Our studio delivers a multidisciplinary experience through the creation and development of concepts, identities, products, graphics, and interiors. Along with the five collections/projects we launch each year, we create various works and commissions and act as design consultants and curators. Our work has been featured in some of the world's most prestigious exhibitions and is part of the permanent collection of the Victoria and Albert Museum in London, England. Our studio is based in Eidenhoven, Netherlands.

www.bcxsy.com

"Our main inspirations for the pieces made in South Africa were the beads themselves—their bright colors—and the old ceramic technique of coiling."

A *Coiled Vase (Small)*, 2010
20 x 12 cm
Czech glass beads, recycled plastic bottle, recycled fabric; made by Thokozani Sibisi
Photo by Hironori Tsukue

B *Siyazama Women Holding the Prototypes from the Workshop*, 2010
Lobolile Ximba, Sbongile Ximba, Celani Noyjeza, Princess Ngonephi Ngcobo, Kishwepi Sitole, Tholiwe Sitole, Beauty Ndlovu, and Thokozani Sibisi
Photo by Editions in Craft

A

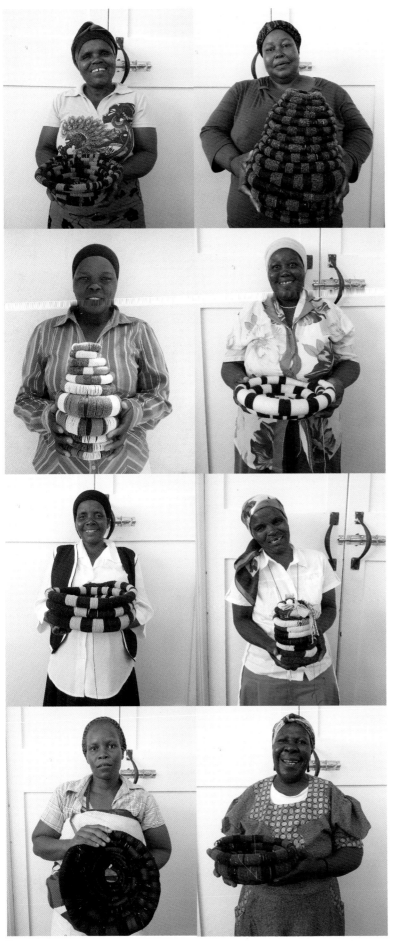

B

YOU RECENTLY COLLABORATED WITH THE SIYAZAMA PROJECT, A COLLECTIVE OF TWENTY WOMEN BEADERS FROM THE RURAL PROVINCE OF KWAZULU-NATAL IN SOUTH AFRICA. HOW DID YOU BECOME INVOLVED WITH THE COLLECTIVE?
The opportunity came about through the invitation of Editions in Craft, an international platform for artists and designers who want to explore the technical and artistic possibilities of traditional crafts. Before the trip, we came up with a design concept that we wanted to see applied and tested by the South African beaders. The idea was to develop a concept that left them with some space to add their personal input instead of just following a strict repetitive design. We spent 10 days in South Africa working with the group.

HOW DID THE WORKING PROCESS GO ONCE THE PROJECT WAS UNDERWAY?
The working process remained quite dynamic throughout our stay. Knowing the theoretical part of a technique is very different from actually practicing it, so we remained open and observed everything that was happening in order to achieve the best results. One of our main objectives was to use only locally available materials. This turned out to be funny, because we learned that beads have never been produced in South Africa—they were always imported. But we tried to include only basic additional materials, such as cloth and plastic bottles. Due to the short time frame we had for the project, we were actually working on the pieces up until the last moment, before leaving for the airport.

WHAT INSPIRED YOUR DESIGN CONCEPT?

Our inspiration came from various places. The bigger beaded surfaces remind us of the skin of serpents. When these pieces are viewed from a distance, it's sometimes difficult to tell what the surface is made of. Another inspiration was the old method of coiling that's used to create ceramic vessels. We find it interesting that a long, rounded element can be used to create a voluminous, three-dimensional object.

WHAT ARE YOUR FAVORITE ASPECTS OF THE PIECES IN THE COLLECTION?

We really like the visual effect of the massive, rounded, beaded surfaces. We're happy that each of the vases looks different depending on the person who made it. Each vase is different, and yet each one has general characteristics that make it recognizable as part of the collection.

WHAT RESPONSES HAVE YOU GOTTEN TO THE WORK?

We were very happy to hear the ladies' responses to the project. Many of them were glad to do something they'd never done

A

B

C

D

A *Coiled Lamp*, 2010
175 cm
Traditional Czech glass beads, fabric,
electrical cord; made by Beauty Ndlovu
Photo by Hironori Tsukue

B *Coiled Vase (Medium)*, 2010
27 x 16 cm
Traditional Czech glass beads, fabric,
plastic bottle; made by Princess
Ngonephi Ngcobo
Photo by Hironori Tsukue

C *Celani Noyjeza Making a Coiled
Vase*, 2010
Photo by Editions in Craft

D *Coiled Vase (Large)*, 2010
30 x 24 cm
Traditional Czech glass beads, fabric,
plastic bottle; made by Lobolile Ximba
Photo by Hironori Tsukue

before and to have the chance to influence the pieces they were working on. Responses from the general public have been warm. People like the looks of the work but are also interested in the process and background of the project.

**DO YOU PLAN TO
USE BEADS AGAIN
IN FUTURE WORK?**
Working with beads for this project was a very positive experience, and we think that they offer many possibilities. We'd be happy to do another project with them if the opportunity arises. Since we like working and experimenting with different techniques, it's hard to say when that will happen.

**CAN YOU TELL US ABOUT
SOME FUTURE PROJECTS
YOU HAVE PLANNED?**
We're currently working on a glass project in Osaka, Japan, that will be launched during Tokyo Design Week. We're looking into the possibilities of other collaborative projects in Japan. A textile commission in which we're experimenting with embroidery is also keeping us busy.

"It would never occur to me to fashion vases from beads and rags—how clever!"

—SUZANNE GOLDEN

colleen o'rourke

"Color is my motivator."

I live in Grand Rapids, Michigan. I was born into an artistic family, and imagination was encouraged at an early age. I was taught not only to appreciate art, but also to generate it. This early support allowed me the ability to trust my artistic instincts and embrace the creative process. I like the challenge that beading offers with a limited color palette and minuscule size. I find the process of this medium to be intimate and meditative. My bead pieces are narratives. One viewer may see joy and peace in a particular work that another viewer sees as disturbing and full of angst. I want the viewer to walk away still thinking about my pieces and instead of wondering what I was trying to convey, let them be relevant to their own reality.

www.corourke.com

A

A *Worm's-Eye View*, 2011
38.1 x 38.1 cm
Seed beads, thread, cotton
fabric; bead embroidery
Photo by artist

B *Jerry's Day Out*, 2008
22.9 x 22.9 cm
Seed beads, thread, cotton
fabric; bead embroidery
Photo by artist

C *Loretta's Night In*, 1999
22.9 x 22.9 cm
Seed beads, thread, cotton
fabric; bead embroidery
Photo by artist

B

C

HOW DO YOU CHOOSE YOUR IMAGERY? DOES YOUR WORK HAVE A NARRATIVE?

When ideas come to me, I sketch them out. Sometimes they work, and sometimes they don't. I believe that all of my beadwork is narrative. I like it when the viewer can narrate a piece so that it suits his or her life.

HOW WOULD YOU DESCRIBE YOUR WORK?

My work is neurotic—sarcastic, sardonic, acerbic, and occasionally pretty. It relates directly to my life. Whether it's a moment, a thought, or an actual occurrence, there's a bit of a self-portrait in each piece.

WHY BEADS RATHER THAN PAINT, PASTELS, OR PENCIL?

Beads are an obsession. Once a person starts working with them, it's difficult to stop. I do paint, but painting is an entirely different process. My paintings don't resemble my beadwork at all. I truly enjoy both mediums. Because painting and beadwork provoke different sensations and restrictions, and therefore different ideas and emotions, my mood dictates which medium I'll work in at any given time.

TELL US HOW EACH PIECE COMES ABOUT.

I plan out my designs on paper, then I figure out which color will go where. This can be a long process, because if I put down a color that doesn't work, I have to rip it out. I typically stretch a piece of fabric over stretcher bars and sketch the design onto the fabric. The composition tends to stay true to the sketch, but the work definitely evolves as I go.

HAS THIS PROCESS CHANGED OVER TIME?

Since I began working with beads, I've tried to experiment with color and light. I've used several different types of beads and discovered that my favorites are opaque seed beads. I've learned that if you lay these beads down in one direction, you'll get an entirely different look from them than if you lay them down in the opposite direction. They could be the same exact color, but by changing their direction, they catch the light differently and produce different hues. Size matters. I mostly use size 11 and occasionally size 10. These sizes let me create detailed work.

HOW WERE YOU INTRODUCED TO BEADING?

During the summer of 1991, at the University of Michigan School of Art and Design, I took a glassblowing workshop. My teacher and the guest artist in the adjacent room decided to switch students for a day. That day changed my life and my work, because I was introduced to beading by the amazing Joyce Scott.

A

B

A *Mom, Just Resting Her Eyes,* 1999
25.4 x 25.4 cm
Seed beads, thread, adhesive, wood; peyote stitch
Photo by artist

B *At the Lake,* 2004
16.5 x 21.6 cm
Seed beads, thread, cotton fabric; bead embroidery
Photo by artist

C *On the Town,* 2006
38.1 x 27.9 cm
Seed beads, thread, cotton fabric; bead embroidery
From the private collection of Michael Walsh Wolfe
Photo by artist

C

A

A *Elvis Christ*, 1998
17.8 x 12.7 cm
Seed beads, thread, adhesive,
acid-free mat board
Photo by Kevin O'Rourke

B *In*, 2010
30.5 x 25.4 cm
Seed beads, thread, cotton
fabric; bead embroidery
Photo by artist

C *Bedtime Stories*, 2001
31.8 x 47 cm
Seed beads, thread, cotton
fabric; bead embroidery
From the private collection of
Rebecca Sive
Photo by artist

B

C

WHAT RESPONSES DO YOU GET TO YOUR WORK?

Most people respond with the questions, "How long did this take you?" and "How many beads did you use?" These are valid questions, but they're impossible for me to answer precisely. If I had to guess, I'd say that I spend one to three hours per square inch (2.5 cm), depending on the detail. As for how many beads, I'd say approximately 250 per square inch (2.5 cm).

"There's more than meets the eye in Colleen's work. At first glance, the simplicity belies what closer inspection reveals."
—SUZANNE GOLDEN

felieke
van der leest

Born in Emmen, Nether-
lands, I grew up near a
zoo and developed a pas-
sion for animals early in
life. My interest in textile
techniques also started at
an early age. In college, I
trained as a metalsmith,
graduating in 1996 from the
jewelry department of the
Gerrit Rietveld Academy of
Fine Arts in Amsterdam. In
2008, I moved to the small
Norwegian village of Øys-
tese, where I now live with
my husband, Jan, and son,
Felix. I collect plastic toy
animals and own more than
1,000 of them. In an effort
to improve my Norwegian-
language skills, I sing in a
local choir. I love to garden.
I exhibit my work regularly
and am represented by
galleries in Amsterdam,
New York, and Tokyo.

www.feliekevanderleest.com

A

A *The End I (Brooch)*, 2011
12 x 11 x 4 cm
Seed beads, plastic animal, silver,
leather; bead embroidery, metalwork
Photo by Eddo Hartmann

B *Gusz Goosz (Necklace)*, 2006
Hanging goose: 12.5 x 4.5 x 4.5 cm
Gold, textile, seed beads, plastic toy,
topaz; bead crochet, metalwork
Photo by Eddo Hartmann

B

"Beads are like little bricks—you can build with them and make the most beautiful patterns."

That is for others to do. I have no idea—I just create.

WELL, TELL US ABOUT THIS PROCESS.
I usually start with an idea about a particular animal. I get a picture in my head and start working directly or make a sketch so I don't forget the idea. While I'm working, I try to get a sense of whether or not the idea is as good in reality as it is in my head. There's a lot of change and evolution involved, but that's okay. The most important thing is to start—the work tells the story. If I get a bad feeling or find myself in a bad mood, I know that I'm heading in the wrong direction. Sometimes I put the work aside for a while and wait. Then, suddenly, I might think of a good solution to the "problem" with the piece or recognize what it is I need to change. These days, it takes a lot of time to develop a new work. I often write down new patterns or how-to descriptions so I can repeat them.

WHAT INSPIRES YOUR WORK?

I think I've been inspired by everything that surrounded me from the moment I was born. Now I'm surrounded by hundreds of plastic toy animals that give me ideas. Inspiration can come at any moment. Sometimes I have no ideas for a while, which can be a bit scary. But then the ideas start to flow again, one after the other. I love those times!

WHAT RESPONSES DO YOU GET TO YOUR WORK?

I get very positive responses. My work is figurative, colorful, and often humorous. Children love it and sometimes recognize the animals.

WHEN AND HOW DID YOU BEGIN BEADING?

When I was a child, I had a beadweaving period, but I was impatient and didn't know what to do with all the vertical threads I ended up with. I also crocheted with beads, which perfectly combined my love for crochet and my love for seed beads. And I've always been fascinated by the beadwork of North American Indians.

A

B

A *Sir Beauty B. Dandy*, 2008
22 x 18 x 11 cm
Plastic toy, gold-plated silver, silver, seed beads, hair, textile, cubic zirconia; oxidized, metalwork, bead crochet
Photo by Eddo Hartmann

B *McPufff (Brooch)*, 2009
9.5 x 9.5 x 3.5 cm
Textile, gold, plastic toy, seed beads, cubic zirconia; bead crochet, metalwork, beadweaving
Photo by Eddo Hartmann

C

D

E

C *Soccer Baby (Ring)*, 2008
7.5 x 5.5 x 5 cm
Seed beads, gold, plastic toy,
textile, leather, silver, cubic zirconia;
bead embroidery, metalwork
Photo by Eddo Hartmann

D & E *Game of the Cheetahs
(Necklace)*, 2008
32 x 25 x 2.5 cm
Seed beads, textile, plastic toys,
silver, gold; oxidized, beadweaving,
bead crochet, metalwork
Photos by Eddo Hartmann

HOW HAS YOUR USE OF BEADS EVOLVED?

I have worked with seed beads throughout my career, but in the past couple of years I have used them more. I used to buy them from bead shops in Amsterdam, but they didn't have a large selection and the quality was also not so good for small and precise work. In 2005 I discovered how to order them through the Internet, where there is a wider selection. I use seed beads to add a new texture to the work. I could crochet those parts only with yarn, but sometimes there's just too much textile and the work needs another material.

A *Squaw Kitten (Rings)*, 2011
Each: 12 x 7.5 x 0.5 cm
Silver, seed beads, textile; bead
crochet, metalwork
Photo by Eddo Hartmann

B *Yellow Kelly (Necklace)*, 2008
Canary: 10 x 10 x 3.5 cm
Seed beads, textile, gold, plastic toy,
cubic zirconia; metalwork,
bead crochet
Photo by Eddo Hartmann

C *Peace Parrot (Brooch)*, 2010
14 x 10 x 2.5 cm
Textile, seed beads, gold-plated
metal, plastic toy, gold, cubic
zirconia; bead crochet
Photo by Eddo Hartmann

D *Spirit of the Cat (Necklace)*, 2011
Pendant: 22 x 7.5 x 2 cm
Seed beads, silver, gold, plastic toy,
topaz; beadweaving, metalwork
Photo by Eddo Hartmann

"I love it when a
sense of humor comes
through in work.
Felieke's clever way
of using beads and
crochet leaves the
viewer smiling."

—SUZANNE GOLDEN

betsy youngquist

I was born in Rockford, Illinois, and still call it home. I discovered beadwork when I was seven and my family went on a summer trip through Canada and Alaska in an Airstream trailer. I still have a pair of moccasins from the trip. I started applying beads to the surfaces of my watercolor paintings more than 20 years ago. Today, I explore the interconnection between man and the natural world through beaded sculptures. During the past dozen years, I've exhibited my work in galleries throughout the United States, including the Smithsonian Institution in Washington, D.C., and the John Michael Kohler Arts Center in Sheboygan, Wisconsin. I have an enduring love for all creatures great and small, and I'm fascinated by the intersection of humans, animals, and mythology—a theme that frequently appears in my work.

www.byart.com

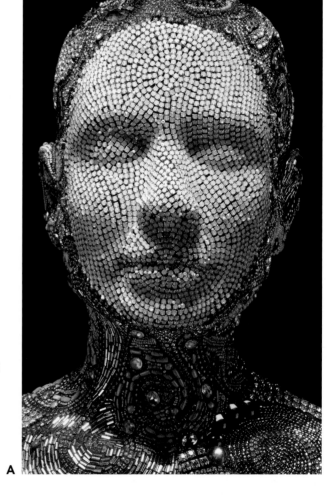

A & B *Metamorphosis*, 2011
117 x 43 x 20 cm
Urethane foam, human glass prosthetic eyes, glass beads, wire, screws, vintage glass stones, shell, coral, adhesives, grout; mosaic
Photos by Larry Sanders

A

"Sometimes I creep to my studio before bed and ask my uncompleted sculptures which beads to use next."

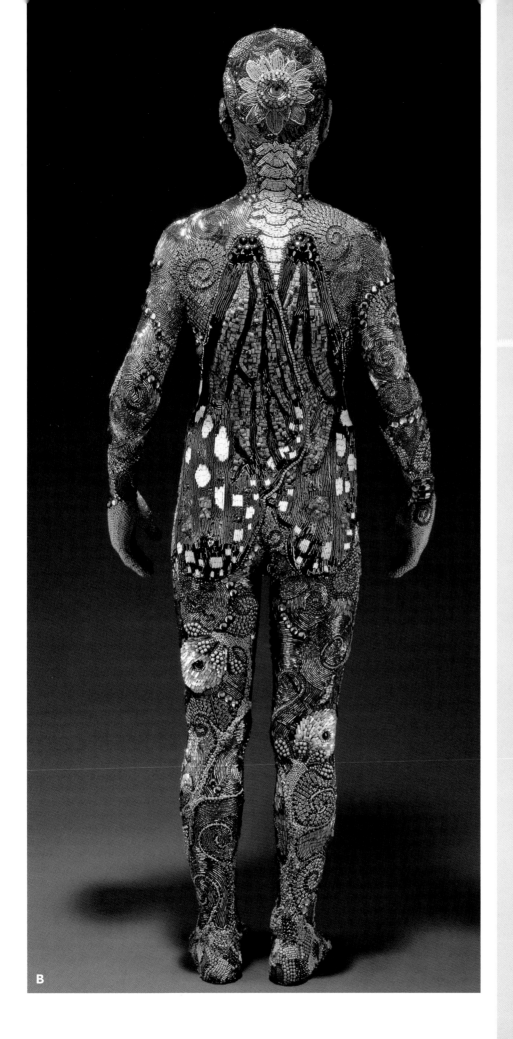

B

DOES YOUR WORK CONTAIN A MESSAGE?

I try to communicate stewardship and a respect for the environment through my work. I view the world as a magical, wonderful, spiritual place. My art helps me maintain, explore, and share that belief. It's a joyful thing.

HOW WOULD YOU DESCRIBE THE WORK?

The easiest description is three-dimensional mixed media. I mix beadwork, sculpture, mosaics, and assemblage. I think the art movement that's most closely connected to my work is Surrealism.

HOW DO YOU MAKE THE PIECES?

I work with my partner, R. Scott Long. First, we break and/or cut antique porcelain doll heads. Then I take some of the pieces and put them together like a puzzle. During this process, I set the eyes. Next, we look at the face and decide what type of animal it's projecting. We then do a sketch, and Scott carves the form. I adhere glass beads, vintage glass stones, porcelain doll parts, and glass eyes to the surface of the form and let it dry. Then I grout the entire piece using a dark tile grout. It's messy, but I love the effect of beads embedded in a dark ground, like dirt. On a good day, I know the next two or three bead choices I'm going to make. I design as I go, and Scott often assists me when I can't figure out which bead to use next.

HOW DO YOU COME UP WITH THE TITLES FOR YOUR PIECES?

A name usually just pops into my head while I'm working. To a certain extent, the personality of each piece directs me. *Dylan* has the personality and look of my godson, so that name was easy, although it didn't surface until I was halfway finished with him. *Beast*, on the other hand, is an exploration of our perceptions concerning the concepts of prey versus predator. The name just popped out of the blue, and I had to figure out its significance. I guess some names are deep and some are as light as a feather. It's my job to catch whatever ideas are buzzing around a piece and connect the dots.

HOW HAS YOUR ART MAKING EVOLVED?

Over the past 20 years, I've gone from working in two dimensions to working in three. When I was finishing college, my watercolor paintings began to feel incomplete, so I glued small bits of colored foil paper to their surfaces. I soon went from foil paper to beads. Their detail and texture allowed me to resolve the unfinished component in my creative process. Years later, after

A

B

A *Beast*, 2005
48 x 91 x 20 cm
Taxidermy form, glass beads, shell, vintage glass stones, human prosthetic glass eyes, adhesives, grout; mosaic
Photo by Larry Sanders

B *Harry*, 2011
20 x 18 x 10 cm
Urethane foam, antique porcelain doll parts, glass doll eyes, glass beads, vintage glass stones, adhesives, grout; mosaic
Photo by Larry Sanders

C *Masquerade*, 2004
43 x 30 x 15 cm
Taxidermy form, taxidermy eyes, glass beads, glass vintage stones, adhesives, grout; mosaic
Photo by Larry Sanders

D *Dylan*, 2010
30 x 18 x 13 cm
Urethane foam, antique porcelain doll parts, glass doll eyes, glass beads, shell, vintage glass stones, brass bugle beads, adhesives, grout; mosaic
Photo by Larry Sanders

E *Otto*, 2010
28 x 18 x 43 cm
Urethane foam, antique porcelain doll parts, glass human prosthetic eyes, glass beads, vintage glass stones, adhesives, grout; mosaic
Photos by Larry Sanders

C

D

E

A *Woody*, 2009
28 x 25 x 15 cm
Urethane foam, antique porcelain doll parts, human glass prosthetic eyes, glass beads, vintage glass stones, shell, adhesives, grout; mosaic
Photo by Larry Sanders

B *No. 54*, 2010
30 x 38 x 18 cm
Urethane foam, antique porcelain doll parts, glass doll eyes, glass beads, vintage glass stones, shell, adhesives, grout; mosaic
Photos by Larry Sanders

C *Tricky Dog*, 2009
20 x 15 x 8 cm
Urethane foam, antique porcelain doll parts, glass doll eyes, glass beads, coral, vintage glass stones, adhesives, grout; mosaic
Photo by Larry Sanders

D *Tweet Tweet*, 2007
18 x 25 x 13 cm
Urethane foam, antique porcelain doll parts, glass doll eyes, glass beads, shell, vintage glass stones, adhesives, grout; mosaic
Photo by Larry Sanders

C

D

teaching teenagers how to make mosaics for a summer program, I was inspired to try the mosaic process with beads. In 2004, I ordered a rabbit taxidermy form and covered it in beads. I was upset about not being accepted into a show and decided to make something just for myself. That rabbit was my leap from two- to three-dimensional work. It ended up on the cover of *American Style* magazine and was used in the publicity for the Smithsonian Craft Show in 2005.

WHAT RESPONSES DO YOU GET TO YOUR WORK? Joy is a common response. But not everyone responds well to what I do. I've had encounters with people who find the narrative content of my work disturbing. There's something good about walking that tightrope. If everyone liked or was indifferent to what I did, it wouldn't feel quite right.

"Betsy posts images online showing the progression of the creation of her magical creatures. It's a fascinating process to watch."

—SUZANNE GOLDEN

estyn hulbert

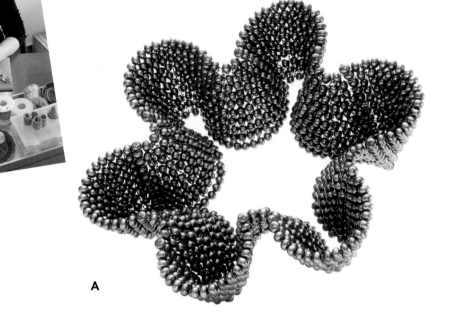

A

I was born in Edinburgh, Scotland, but spent my early childhood in France and Switzerland. I've been working with beads since I was a kid. As a student I returned to Scotland and enrolled in the Edinburgh College of Art, where I studied photography, graphic design, and animation. In 2000, I moved to New York City. Five years later, I launched my own jewelry line. I now live in a nineteenth-century farmhouse in the village of Ellenville, New York. My studio is surrounded by mountains, a vegetable garden, and an old barn with raccoon paw prints on the walls. I love nature and am inspired by growing things, geometric shapes, typography, ancient symbols, scraps of lace, shells, and driftwood found on the beach.

www.estynhulbert.com

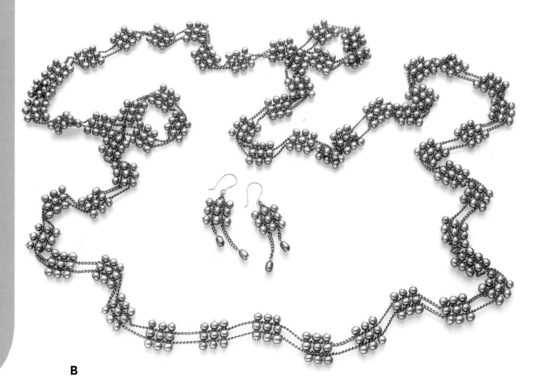

B

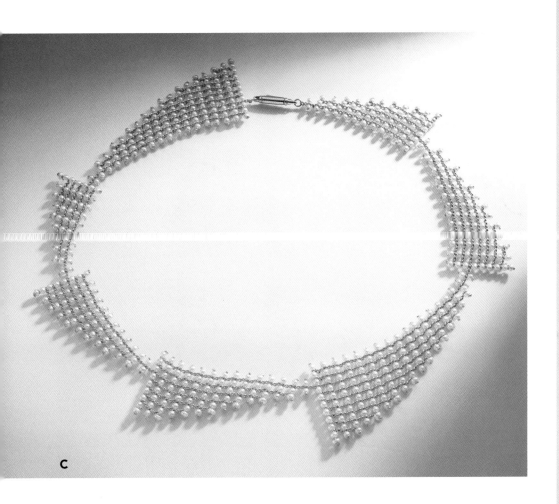

C

"Beads are units, like bricks or stitches, and you can build almost anything with them. There's no end to their potential."

A *Flower Cuff*, 2009
10 x 10 x 4 cm
Pearls, chain, wire;
personal technique
Photo by Ralph Gabriner

B *Long Squares Necklace* and *Square Earrings*, 2008
Necklace: 1.3 x 122 cm
Earrings: 4 x 1.25 cm each
Pearls, chain, wire;
personal technique
Photo by Ralph Gabriner

C *Deco Choker*, 2008
4 x 43 x 4 cm
Pearls, chain, wire;
personal technique
Photo by Ralph Gabriner

**IS THERE MUCH PLAN-
NING INVOLVED IN YOUR
WORKING PROCESS,
OR DO YOU DESIGN
AS YOU BEAD?**

I sketch ideas as they
come to me, frequently
on the backs of enve-
lopes. Once in a while,
I corral my ideas into a
sketchbook. I'm fastidi-
ous about dating every-
thing and sometimes
find that I've drawn
the same idea multiple
times over a period of
years. Apparently, ideas
will keep asserting
themselves until they
get made. I have to ac-
tually make a piece to
find out whether it will
work. I can't always
anticipate the effects
of gravity and geom-
etry on the object
I'm building.

**HOW HAS YOUR WORK-
ING PROCESS EVOLVED
OVER TIME?**

I've come to trust my
working process more
and more. I recognize
the way it feels when
an idea has potential,
and I follow that feeling
by attempting to build
the piece. Sometimes a
piece works right away.
Other times, I might hit
a technical roadblock and
let the test sample sit on
my desk—sometimes
for months—until I
pick it up again and
try a different way of

A

B

A *Elizabethan Choker*, 2008
5 x 47 cm
Pearls, chain, wire
Photo by Ralph Gabriner

B *Cones Choker*, 2008
3 x 43 x 3 cm
Pearls, chain, wire
Photo by Ralph Gabriner

C *Flower Cuff*, 2008
10 x 10 x 4 cm
Pearls, chain, wire
Photo by Ralph Gabriner

C

D *Constellation Necklace*, 2008
2.5 x 81 cm
Pearls, chain, wire
Photo by Ralph Gabriner

E *Circle Drop Earrings*, 2008
Each: 6.25 x 3 cm
Pearls, chain, wire
Photo by Ralph Gabriner

F *Wild Geese Bracelet*, 2008
3.5 x 18.5 cm
Pearls, chain, wire
Photo by Ralph Gabriner

E

making it. Some of the pieces on my desk now may never be solved, but having them in the corner of my eye lets my brain work on the problem subconsciously. Sometimes the problem with one design turns out to be the solution for another.

IS THERE A REASON YOU CHOOSE A MONO-CHROMATIC PALETTE?
I make work in a wide range of colors, both stone and pearl, but I love the simplicity and elegance of white or black pearls. When I'm designing, I like to start by making a sample in white pearls. White allows me to see the structure very clearly while I'm figuring things out.

"I love how Estyn's jewelry is so ethereal. Even in the photos it looks weightless."
—SUZANNE GOLDEN

helena markonsalo

I was born in Mikkeli, Finland, a small town with a strong military history. When I was young, the atmosphere there was conformist and conservative—not the best environment for a sensitive, artistic girl—so I moved away as a teenager. I studied in other cities, including London, where I was a student of jewelry design at the Royal College of Art. In 2002, I spent two months in Benin, West Africa, as an artist in residence in a small village. That time was really important to me because I discovered new ways of looking at jewelry. I now live in Helsinki with my two young daughters, Mango and Saga, and my partner, who's also an artist. I work at home so that I can be with my children. Their world and way of seeing things are big inspirations to me.

www.mer.fi

A

"Beads are my paint, and the needle is my brush."

B

A *Wonderbaum*, 2001
18 x 30 x 3 cm
Copper, enamel, plastic
beads, glass beads, plastic,
thread; sewn
Photo by Magnus Scharmanoff

B *Mr. Vitiligo*, 2011
80 x 80 x 15 cm
Plastic beads, plastic hand, glass
beads, thread, paint; sewn
Photos by Kalle Kataila

WHEN AND HOW DID YOU BEGIN WORKING WITH BEADS?
In 1995 I was an exchange student at London Guildhall University. I lived in East London, where there are many people from Bangladesh and India. East London during that time was a huge experience for me, a young Finnish design student! That's where I discovered beads and color.

DESCRIBE YOUR WORK.
I'm really interested in "do-it-yourself" art, folk art, gothic art, graffiti, and street art, and I believe this is visible in my work. My pieces are combinations of ready-made objects, recycled materials, and second-hand treasures. In my work, there's a fine line between beauty and ugliness, humor and horror. I look for contrasts between ideas and materials. It would be too easy to make nice, pretty art with the materials that I use. I add ugly ingredients to the mix to create contrasts.

HOW DO YOU MAKE THESE PIECES?
Although my art is mostly inspired by personal experience, the materials sometimes lead the way. The materials find me and find their place in my art.

A

A *Club Cool,* 2010
110 x 155 x 2 cm
Textiles, paint, plastic beads,
glass beads, thread; sewn
Photo by Kalle Kataila

B *The Nightmare,* 2008
50 x 50 x 10 cm
Plastic beads, hat, velvet,
chains, thread; sewn
Photo by Kalle Kataila

C *My Little Armour,* 2003
105 x 60 x 5 cm
Dress, plastic beads, earrings,
shells, enamel, copper, chain,
plastic items, paint; sewn
Photos by Rauno Traskelin

B

C

What results is often a surprise. I work in sections, leaving a piece unfinished and continuing it later. That's how I get layers to my work—not only layers of material but also layers of ideas. Because it can take a long time to complete a big piece, my ideas often change as I work. I let this happen freely. I try to use beads like paint or any other kind of material. I'm not interested in beading techniques.

HAS YOUR PROCESS CHANGED OVER TIME?
My work has moved from small, jewelry-like pieces to large wall pieces. The beads are falling away gradually.

WHAT RESPONSES DO YOU GET TO YOUR WORK?
Responses are often strong. People either really like my art or don't like it at all.

WELL, PERSONALLY, I LOVE IT! WHY DO YOU THINK SOME PEOPLE REACT NEGATIVELY? Maybe because my work is not design or art, not craft or jewelry, not textile. It goes against expectations. Jewelry reviewers say "it's too big," art critics think it has "too much craft," while in design it's "complicated and restless." The work emits great power, but it doesn't belong to any category. It needs to find its own place.

"Helena is sort of a grafitti artist spray-painting with beads."
—SUZANNE GOLDEN

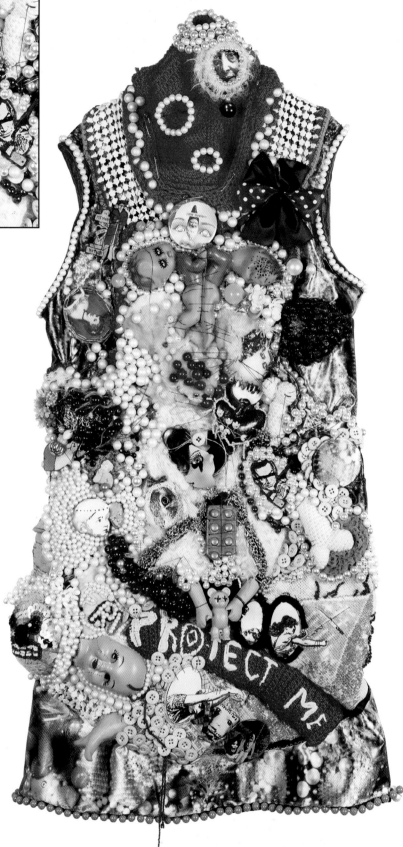

A

B

C

A *Protect Me,* 2009
90 x 50 cm
Fabric, enamel, copper, thread, toys,
beads, buttons, enamel; sewn, knitted
Photos by Kalle Kataila

B *Inbox,* 2010
30 x 60 x 2 cm
Plastic beads, stickers, thread, chain,
metal items, paper, paint; sewn
Photo by Kalle Kataila

C *Limbo Life,* 2006
90 x 160 x 10 cm
Textiles, plastic beads, plastic
earrings, chains, plastic items,
copper, enamel, shells, paint,
glitter, feathers; sewn, knitted
Photo by Kalle Kataila

sari liimatta

I live in Lappeenranta, Finland, where I was born and raised. It's a small town of about 72,000 inhabitants that's located in between the Saimaa archipelago and the border of Russia. My working studio is integrated into my home, which I share with three rabbits and a salamander. Although I've taught before, I prefer to keep my time open and free so that I can work on my art. My pieces are in galleries in Europe and Japan.

www.sariliimatta.net

A *Evolution*, 2010
22 x 21.5 x 7 cm
Glass beads, pins, turquoise, plastic toy
Photo by artist

B *Kingdom*, 2010
5.5 x 34 x 7 cm
Glass beads, self-made brass chain, pins, silver, rubber toy
Photo by artist

B

A

"In my work, I explore how animals were positioned in ancient cultures and how they play a powerful part in our lives today."

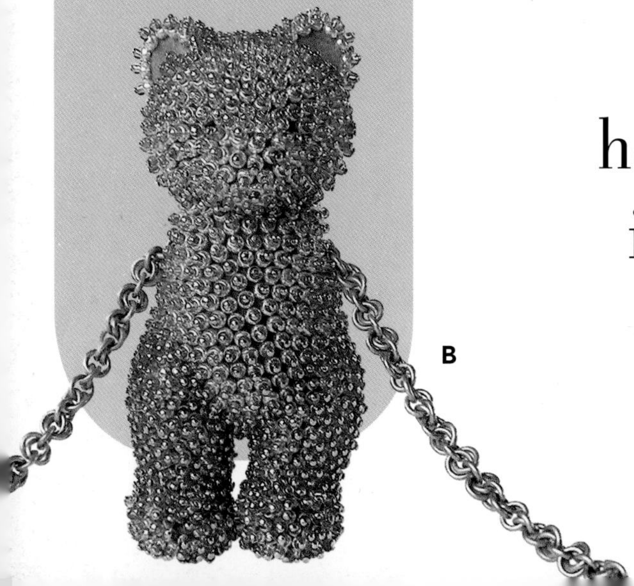

C

E

D

C *Domestication*, 2011
12 x 15.5 x 9 cm
Glass beads, pins, quartz,
polyamide thread, plastic toy
Photo by artist

D *Washed*, 2009
13.5 x 18 x 8 cm
Glass beads, pins, quartzite,
polyamide thread, plastic toy
Photo by artist

E *Sick Sea II*, 2010
9 x 30 x 12 cm
Glass beads, freshwater pearls,
pins, silver, plastic toy
Photo by artist

WHAT'S YOUR FAVORITE PART OF WORKING WITH BEADS?
The moment right before finishing a piece, when you recognize as a true feeling that adding one more super-small bead would be too much. You truly feel that if you added it, it would ruin everything.

DO YOU MAKE YOUR OWN BASES, OR ARE THEY FOUND OBJECTS?
I use found objects as bases because they play an essential part in each story. Each toy animal seems to have its own role. Each one has a distinctive look in his eyes, his own history, his own past, with past users.

HOW WOULD YOU DESCRIBE YOUR WORK?
In my pieces, I use my own voice to tell what has happened to characters—people and animals.

THESE ARE JEWELRY RATHER THAN SCULPTURAL PIECES. WHY DO YOU USE THIS FORMAT?

I often make pieces that I call jewelry sculptures. I think it's possible to study the function of jewelry via both wearable and non-wearable pieces. Wearable pieces have a true connection to the body, but sculptural ones do, too—in the imagination of the viewer.

THE ENDS OF THE PINS ARE VISIBLE IN SOME OF YOUR PIECES. WHY DID YOU LET THEM SHOW?

Sometimes the theme of a piece needs to be told in a very forced manner. Letting the pins show is a way I can do this. It's a tool I use to produce empathy in viewers. It leaves no room for denying the cruelty of life.

HOW DO YOU START A PIECE?

I find a toy animal, which I examine thoroughly to get an idea of how it needs me. Then I connect the toy with a suitable story—it could be something happening around me, or something I saw on TV. It could be a story someone has told me. Next, I search for beads that have the right colors and forms to support and intensify the story.

A

A *Retired*, 2009
14.5 x 17 x 7 cm
Glass beads, crystal, mother-of-pearl, pins, quartz, plastic toy
Photo by artist

B *The Dancing Bear*, 2008
10 x 26 x 8 cm
Glass beads, pins, oxidized silver, plastic toy
Photo by artist

C *Human Effect*, 2011
9.5 x 46 x 11 cm
Glass beads, oxidized silver chain, pins, plastic, polyamide thread
Photo by artist

D *Casual Saints*, 2011
12.5 x 9.5 x 5 cm
Agate, glass beads, pins, plastic toy
Photo by artist

B

C

D

HOW DO YOU CHOOSE THEM?
They have values related to their colors, forms, and materials. They have to fit the story of the piece.

DID ANYONE INTRODUCE YOU TO WORKING WITH BEADS?
I kind of found them by myself. I view them as raw materials, as representatives of materials—glass or stones. I have a stone-smithing background—very technical. When I studied stone smithing, I often felt miserable about destroying a stone's natural form to create something new. Beads give me the opportunity to build a form from particles.

"It's so interesting that Sari appears to use a very straightforward, direct mechanism—pins—to hold the beads on the figures. She's both piercing them and beautifying them."

—SUZANNE GOLDEN

jan huling

After graduating with a degree in design from the Kansas City Art Institute, I worked for many years as a freelance designer producing a wide variety of products, including textiles, dinnerware, packaging, and far too many Santa Claus figurines. I discovered beading around 2001 and quickly become obsessed with it. In 2007, I gave up my day job and dedicated myself to beading. In addition to making art, I write children's books. Home for me is now Hoboken, New Jersey. I consider myself a beadist. My practice is a labor of love.

www.janhuling.com

A *A Tree Grows in Birdland*, 2011
20 x 8 x 14 cm
Wood, ceramic, seed beads, dagger beads, ball chain, metal, twig, glue
Photo by Phil Huling

B *A Gentle Man of Color*, 2010
86 x 40 x 25 cm
Fiberglass mannequin, seed beads, ball chain, tokens, newspaper, feathers, glue
Photo by Phil Huling

A

"I don't plan out my work. I like to be surprised by how a piece evolves organically."

B

HOW WOULD YOU DESCRIBE YOUR WORK?

The *New York Times* referred to it as "oddball assemblage." I like that description.

WHAT RESPONSES DO YOU GET TO IT?

I usually hear "wow!" followed by laughter. I'm often asked how long my pieces take (a long time!) and how my eyesight is (very good, thank you).

WHAT LED TO YOUR PARTICULAR STYLE AND METHOD OF WORKING? DID YOU HAVE A LIGHT-BULB MOMENT?

Because I have a background in surface design, the idea of gluing beaded patterns onto objects appealed to me. I think that the first time I fully realized how transformative my work could be was when I covered a My Little Pony. Covering up all of that powder-blue plastic allowed me to

A

B

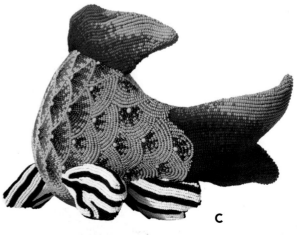

C

A *The Offering*, 2012
38 x 18 x 18 cm
Resin, wood, metal, seed beads,
ball chain, tokens, cabochons, paper,
glass pearl, glue
Photos by Phil Huling

B & C *Lucky*, 2012
15 x 25 x 18 cm
Resin, seed beads, ball chain, glass
cabochons, paper, glass pearl, glue
Photos by Phil Huling

D *Reaching for Enlightenment*, 2006
29 x 13 x 13 cm
Mannequin hand, wood, metal, seed
beads, ball chain, dagger beads, tokens, glue
Photo by Phil Huling

E *Carnivale*, 2012
25 x 13 x 33 cm
Ceramic, paper, seed beads, tokens,
ball chain, cabochons, bugle beads,
glue
Photo by Phil Huling

D

E

see the elegance of the
form itself. That kind of
transformation became
very important to my
way of approaching
a project.

**WHEN AND HOW DID
YOU BEGIN WORKING
WITH BEADS?**
My wonderful, creative
sister, Julie Charles,
came to visit me around
2001. She brought
along a Pez dispenser
that she'd covered in
beads. I thought it was
hilarious and beauti-
ful, and I wanted to
do something similar,
so I started beading
kazoos. I really enjoyed
it! I'd been looking for
a craft that was a good
fit. I'd tried needle-
work, jewelry making,
découpage, and some
other things, but I didn't
feel super inspired by
them. Gluing beads on
stuff just felt right, and
the responses that I got
right from the get-go
were really positive.

**HOW HAS YOUR WORK-
ING PROCESS EVOLVED
OVER TIME?**
I suppose my choice
of objects to cover
has evolved the most.
I started out with
things—boxes, a table,
a shelf—and now have
more fun working on
creatures such as birds,
animals, and dolls.

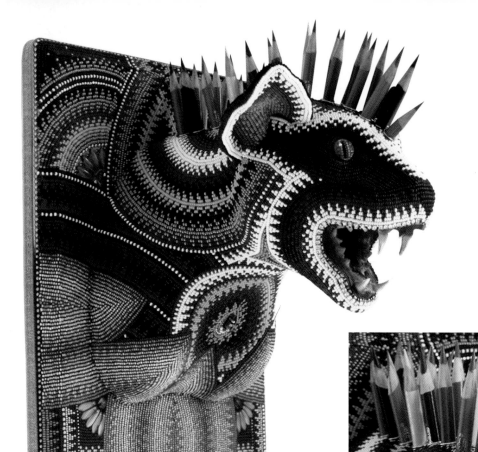

HOW DO YOU CHOOSE THE BEADS YOU USE?

I mostly use 11/0 and 15/0 opaque Czech seed beads, which I often acid etch for a matte finish. The other stuff I use—old buttons, tokens, broken jewelry, crap swept out of junk drawers—is challenging to find, and I'm always on the lookout. I've got boxes of junk that I constantly sift through, so finding new old junk is always exciting for me.

WHAT'S YOUR FAVORITE PART OF WORKING WITH BEADS?

I love finding a new color of seed bead. And I hate that my favorite pink seed beads were discontinued!

"Jan allows her intricate designs to grow organically, eschewing perfection for a more vital and even surprising surface treatment."

—SUZANNE GOLDEN

teresa sullivan

I have a deep love for the surreal and the irreverent. I live in Olympia, Washington, with my husband. Since 1987, I've been making music with him, playing electric bass and sharing vocal duties. My beading studio has always been a desk in the corner of our living room—near the stereo! When the weather is good (weathercasters tell us when to expect "sunbreaks" in the coastal Northwest), I work outdoors. I'm a fan of underground comics, certain Beat Generation and science fiction writers, ethnographic art, envelope-pushers, contrarians, and flat-out weirdos. If I ever get old, I'd like to travel to Morocco, Ghana, Nigeria, and Kenya to meet the people, the music, the beads, and the jewelry.

www.teresasullivanstudio.com

A

"I use a variety of stitches from around the world, each of which gives a different texture and sculptural capability to the work."

B

If He Hollers, 2007
28 x 20 x 3 cm
Glass seed beads, thread;
sculptural hollow-form peyote
stitch, herringbone weave,
ladder stitch
Photo by Dan Kvitka

B *Wanted on Six Planets*,
2008
33 x 18 x 3 cm
Glass seed beads, thread;
sculptural hollow-form peyote
stitch, open-weave netting
Photos by Dan Kvitka

WHAT'S YOUR WORK ABOUT?

Narratives of morphing realities, untamable truths, and the examination of what it takes for people to pass beyond fear.

HOW DO YOU CHOOSE YOUR IMAGERY?

I think of what types of visuals will best support the message while recognizing that I don't need absolute control over how the message is received or interpreted. Some topics are better conveyed as flat, graphic, tapestry images. Others are more suitable as three-dimensional figures or abstract forms.

DESCRIBE HOW YOU WORK. IS THERE MUCH PLANNING INVOLVED, OR DO YOU DESIGN AS YOU MAKE?

I call this process "improvisation with intent." I make larger-scale choices based on theme and format, and continue with hundreds of microdecisions as I work. There's some push and pull between my intent and what I see unfolding before me.

67
SULLIVAN

WHAT INSPIRES YOUR WORK?

The art of Robert Williams, S. Clay Wilson, Richard M. Powers, and Raymond Pettibon. Writers Philip K. Dick, William S. Burroughs, H.P. Lovecraft, and J.G. Ballard. The fearless beadwork of Joyce Scott. When I notice interesting things in my everyday surroundings—clothing details, car grilles, balcony railings—I translate them into weaving structures.

WHAT'S YOUR FAVORITE PART OF WORKING WITH BEADS?

Oddly enough, I like that the process has limitations. You can't blend beads like you can blend paints, and you're working with a given size and shape. But the range of expression is massive. The slow pace of the process gives me time to think as I work. Also, beading is low-tech and nontoxic; you don't need to burn anything. You can create art using only beads, needle, and thread.

A

B

C

A *Silver-Tongued Devil*, 2011
7 x 4 x 4 cm
Glass seed beads, thread; sculptural hollow-form peyote stitch
Photo by artist

B Untitled, 2011
18 x 5 x 5 cm
Glass seed beads, thread; sculptural hollow-form peyote stitch
Photo by artist

D

E

C Untitled, 2009
Average size: 90 x 3 x 3 cm
Glass seed beads, thread; herringbone
weave, sculptural hollow-form peyote
stitch
Photo by Dan Kvitka

D Battle of the Centaurianess, 2004
30 x 12 x 8 cm
Glass seed beads, thread;
sculptural hollow-form
peyote stitch
Photo by Dan Kvitka

E Question, 2007
18 x 10 x 8 cm
Glass seed and bugle beads,
thread; sculptural hollow-form
peyote stitch, open weave
Photo by Dan Kvitka

F Breakthrough, 2007
23 x 13 x 8 cm
Glass seed and bugle beads,
thread; sculptural hollow-form
peyote stitch, open weave
Photo by Dan Kvitka

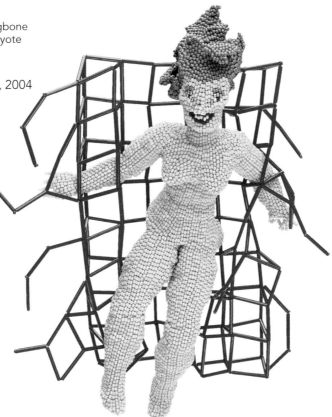

F

WHEN AND HOW DID YOU BEGIN BEADING?

In 1992, three things happened. I was given a bag of wet clay and began making ceramic beads; the drummer of the band I was in gave me some beads that his roommate left behind; and I had my ears pierced. I began trading my ceramic beads for those of a lapidary artist, and he insisted that I join the Portland Bead Society. Joyce Scott gave a slide talk at the society in 1994, and her work galvanized me to embrace beadweaving.

HOW DO YOU CHOOSE BEADS?

The beads have to support the message of the piece. Color is the most important consideration. I'll work with difficult beads if the color is right. I favor Czech seed beads, because their rounded shape is conducive to dimensional work, and I also use Japanese seed beads. Depending on the piece, I'll mix bead sizes and incorporate found materials.

A *Ecstasy*, 2005
41 x 46 x 26 cm
Glass seed beads, thread, artist's
sketch; three-drop peyote stitch
Photo by Dan Kvitka

B Untitled, 2011
13 x 23 x 10 cm
Glass seed beads, thread; sculptural hollow-form peyote stitch
Photos by artist

C *Miami Rice*, 2008
43 x 20 x 3 cm
Glass seed beads, thread; peyote
stitch, right angle weave
Photo by Dan Kvitka

C

TELL US ABOUT THE STITCHES YOU USE.
I use a wide variety of stitches from around the world. Each one gives different textures and sculptural capabilities to the work. Peyote or gourd stitch allows me to create dense, structurally sound artworks that have intricate details and specific shaping. I form hexagon, diamond, and irregular shapes in two and three dimensions with netting and other open weaves. Ndbele weave has a distinctive chevron pattern, and like the other stitches, it's adapted for both two- and three-dimensional work. Right angle weave gives me control of the flexibility of the beaded fabric, from very supple to completely stiff.

"I remember my reaction the first time I saw Teresa's *Ecstasy* necklace. I wanted to be that good, and then I wanted to own it and wear it."

—SUZANNE GOLDEN

linda dolack

I live in the tiny town of Kiel, Wisconsin, with my husband, Tom, and our rescue dogs, Frank and Walter. I hold a BFA from Barat College in Lake Forest, Illinois, and an MFA from the School of the Art Institute of Chicago. I've never tasted a Twinkie, but I've beaded a box of them. In addition to beaded foods, I create embellished fiberglass sculptures for children's hospitals and public art events. My rhinestone cows have been featured in Chicago, New York, and Houston. In my opinion, almost anything will benefit from a liberal application of beads. My dogs worry that they'll be next.

www.lindadolack.com

A

"I love that no matter who sees my work, there's recognition and often a great story connected to a specific food."

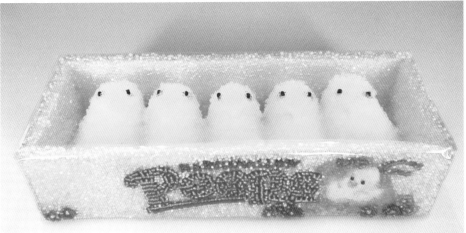

B

A Untitled, 2001
Various dimensions
Seed and bugle beads,
rhinestones, adhesive,
paperboard boxes, mixed
media; hand applied
Photos by artist

B *Peeps®*, 2012
3.8 x 17.8 x 6.4 cm
Glass seed beads,
vintage rhinestones,
paperboard box, cel-
lophane, acrylic paint,
mixed media
Photos by artist

C *Mallomars®*, 1997
5.1 x 23.5 x 11.4 cm
Glass seed beads,
paperboard box, mixed media
Photo by artist

HOW DID YOU GET INTO BEADING?

I hold a BFA in painting and photography but suffer from allergies to many of the chemicals involved with these mediums. So, after earning my degree, I started a hand-weaving business. Weaving seemed safe. The colors and textures of the materials were a plus, but I wasn't able to fulfill all of my creative ideas through weaving. That's when NanC Meinhardt, a friend and beader, suggested I explore beads. I laugh when I re-member telling her I'd never use them! A class in embel-lishment taught by Darrel Morris at the School of the Art Institute of Chicago be-came the missing link and a perfect fit!

DESCRIBE YOUR WORK.

Divine excess! Embellished to the max, it's happy work that functions on several levels.

WHY DO YOU BEAD THE TYPE OF OBJECTS THAT YOU DO?

Junk foods are unhealthy but ever present, and yet I'm fascinated by them! As objects, food containers are exciting. Saturated with col-or, bold graphics, and logos, they foster a desire for and a devotion to specific products. Food is the most ubiquitous commodity of our daily lives.

A *Domino Dots® Sugar Bowl* and *Dean's Milk Chug® Creamer*, 2008
Bowl: 16.5 x 15.2 x 6.4 cm
Creamer: 20.3 x 12.1 x 4.4 cm
Glass seed and bugle beads, vintage jewelry, rhinestones, adhesive, cardboard and plastic containers, wood, mixed media
Photo by artist

B *Lipton® Teapot with Teabag*, 2006
31.8 x 25.4 cm
Glass seed and bugle beads, rhinestones, sequins, cardboard container, adhesive, plastic, wood, acrylic paint, mixed media; hand sewn, hand applied
Photo by artist

C *Red Bull®* and *Sugarless Red Bull® Goblets*, 2007
Each: 25.4 x 5.1 cm
Aluminum cans, wood, glass seed and bugle beads, rhinestones, acrylic paint, adhesive
Photo courtesy of the Mobilia Gallery, Cambridge, Massachusetts
In the collection of the Museum of Arts and Design, New York

D

E

F

D *Vienna Chicago Style Relish®, Heinz Ketchup®, Wonder Hot Dog Buns®, and French's Mustard®*, 2003
Relish: 13.3 x 7.6; ketchup: 21.6 x 6.4;
buns: 7 x 20.3 x 24.5 cm;
mustard: 11.4 x 7.6
Glass seed and bugle beads,
adhesive, sequins, glass bottles
and jars, plastic, marble paste, mixed
media; hand sewn, hand applied
Photo by artist

E *Fluff®*, 2003
14 x 7.6 cm
Glass seed and bugle beads, cotton,
adhesive, glass jar, acrylic paint, mixed
media; hand sewn, hand applied
Courtesy of the Mobilia Gallery,
Cambridge, Massachusetts
Photo by Emily Garfield

F *Hot Dog Basket*, 2008
11.4 x 27.9 x 20.3 cm
Glass seed and bugle beads, plastic
basket, marble paste, acrylic paint,
mixed media; off-loom hand woven,
hand applied, hand sewn
Photo by artist

G *Mobile Shrine*, 1995
61 x 104.1 x 104.1 cm
Steel grocery cart, plastic beads, metal,
plastic, and vinyl charms, wire, electric
lights, candles, mixed media
Photo by artist

G

WILL YOU TELL US A LITTLE ABOUT HOW YOU MAKE A PIECE?

Once a particular food is chosen, there is some planning, but I would hate to know every single color ahead of time! An element of spontaneity—using what seems best at a particular moment—helps. Containers such as paperboard boxes are reinforced so that they'll stand up to an application of heavy beads. Whenever hand sewing is possible, cotton is used as the foundation. I sandwich some part or all of a label within each piece, so that it becomes a time capsule of sorts. Color choice is generally dictated by individual product design, but I employ as many bright colors and different styles of beads as I can. When it's completed, the artwork should replicate the feel and look of the original food as closely as possible. I always include bar codes.

HOW DO YOU CHOOSE THE BEADS YOU USE?

Details like words and logos are difficult to reproduce, so the smaller the beads, the better. I generally use Czech glass beads, preferring the imperfect cuts to identical beads. Normally, I use nothing larger than a size 10.

"Does food taste better or is it more appealing because of the way it's packaged? I would want to taste all the food Linda has depicted in her work."

—SUZANNE GOLDEN

ceaser nhlenhe mkhize & mildred thafa dlamini

We live in Durban, South Africa. We met in 1997 and are both largely self-taught artists. Ceaser is also a musician. He plays the guitar and choreographs dances. We collaborate on our beaded pieces and have exhibited our work in Europe and the United States. Five of our pieces decorate the judges' chambers at the New Constitutional Court in Johannesburg.

A

"For us, beading is a calling because beads also heal spiritually. There are certain colors, like red and white, which chase away evil spirits. Spiritual healers called *izangoma* wear certain colors of beads for spiritual purposes."

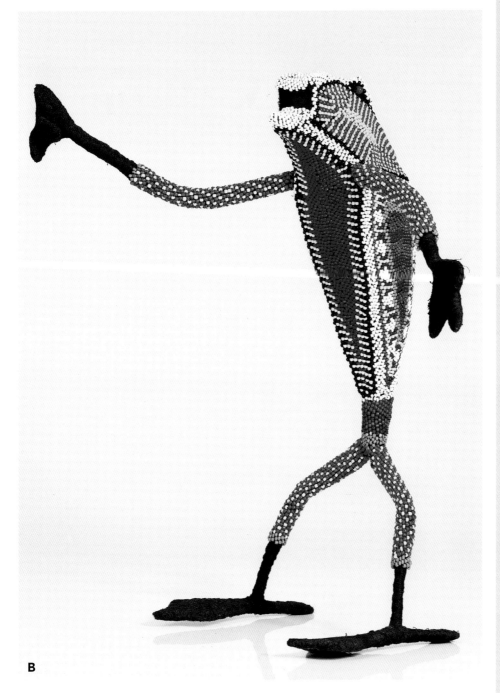

B

C

WHEN AND HOW DID YOU BEGIN BEADING?

Ceaser: In 1999, I attended a workshop at the Durban Art Gallery in South Africa. It was a doll-making workshop specializing in beadwork with dolls. It was open to everybody. That's where I got inspired to do beadwork.

Thafa: When Ceaser came home from that doll-making workshop, he had a packet of mixed beads in his pocket. He laid it on a table. I saw that packet later. I lifted it up and watched it. I saw the beautiful colored beads mixing together and imagined beautiful things. I was alone and bored and felt like trying something with them. I'd never beaded before, but I was used to wearing beads because they're part of our culture. At first, I tried to make bracelets and armbands, but I failed many times. After three days, I came up with a beautiful bracelet, but it didn't impress me because I didn't know anything. I didn't show anyone, not even Ceaser, because I thought he'd laugh at me. I hid it under the bed and kept quiet. A week later, I took the bracelet out unexpectedly and Ceaser saw it. He was very happy with it. He told me he would make a structure that the beaded pattern could cover because the embroidery was unique—no one had ever made it before. So he designed a steel-wire structure of a bird with a tail, one leg, and no wings.

HOW DO YOU DESCRIBE YOUR WORK?

Thafa: I describe it as contemporary African art. It's different from the art made by the people in our country and around the world. No one else makes it. In our country, there are two purposes for beadwork: it's worn, and it's used as decoration. We make decorations in the form of structural animals with our own designs.

WHAT INSPIRES YOUR WORK?

Ceaser: Our work is motivated by a desire to exchange ideas, to encourage debate, and to analyze stereotypes about nature and the environment, especially animals. For example, some cultures associate animals like frogs, owls, and baboons with witchcraft. If those animals are in trouble, people won't help them. So to decorate those animals in our work helps wipe away those rumors.

WHAT'S YOUR WORKING PROCESS LIKE?

Thafa: Our process takes time, partly because we have to thread very small beads. The process depends on the shape of the structure we're making. We base our work on animal forms. We can complete a small piece in about a week. A medium item can take up to two weeks, and a big item

A *Sobohla Manyosi*, 2009
46 x 1.5 cm
Fabric, cotton, wool, steel wire, glass beads
Photo by Graham Carruthers

B *Model C*, 2010
54 x 4 cm
Fabric, cotton, wool, glass beads
Photo by Graham Carruthers

C *Tallest Pride*, 2009
51x 2 cm
Fabric, cotton, wool, steel wire, glass beads
Photo by Graham Carruthers

A

B   C

D

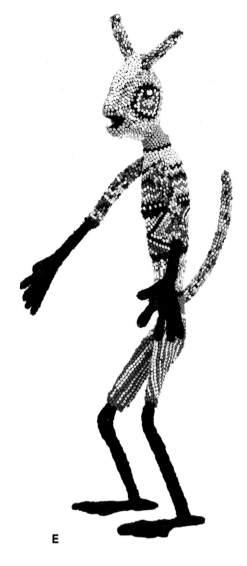

E

F

G

D *Camel*, 2005
39 x 4 cm
Fabric, cotton, wool, steel
wire, glass beads
Photo by Graham Carruthers

E *Hustler*, 2009
45 x 1 cm
Cotton, wool, glass beads,
steel wire
Photo by Graham Carruthers

F *Elephant Man*, 2009
38 x 6 cm
Fabric, cotton, wool, steel
wire, glass beads
Photo by Graham Carruthers

G *Gorilla*, 2004
39 x 6 cm
Cotton, wool, glass beads
Photo by Graham Carruthers

A

B

C

A *Tall Man*, 2007
56 x 3 cm
Fabric, cotton, wool, steel wire,
glass beads
Photo by Graham Carruthers

B *Stranger Bird*, 2005
40 x 50 cm
Cotton, wool, glass beads
Photo by Graham Carruthers

C *Big Frog*, 2002
21 x 38 x 10 cm
Cotton, wool, glass beads,
steel wire
Photo by Graham Carruthers

D *Bum Bum*, 2009
43 x 3 cm
Fabric, cotton, wool, steel
wire, glass beads
Photo by Graham Carruthers

E *Lion*, 2012
16 x 23 x 2 cm
Fabric, cotton, wool,
glass beads, steel wire
Photo by Graham Carruthers

D

E

can take a month or more. The television is always on while we work, so sometimes we use color reflections from the TV. In our culture, we have our own way of decorating. It's based on matching the colors the way our tribes do. Ceaser and I come from the Zulu tribe, which has its own traditional practices. Zulu colors are white, green, red, black, navy, and yellow. We have to follow these colors if our work is to be based on traditional designs. If we freestyle with modern or contemporary art, we don't have to follow these traditional procedures.

WHAT RESPONSES DO YOU GET TO YOUR WORK?
Thafa: Beadwork in our country is usually done by old women, not young people or men. We are young, and Ceaser is a man. People are surprised by this. We thought that maybe we were breaking the rules. But there are people who admire our artwork and don't care about the details. People really communicate with our work. Since we came into the art of beading, everything has changed. Beaders were once underrated. We changed that concept.

"I think this is a terrific interpretation of African beadwork, full of whimsy and fun."
—SUZANNE GOLDEN

kay dolezal

A

I left the field of social work in 1986 to support myself with a "day job," so I could devote my time and energies to learning about fiber art. It was the best decision I ever made, although not the wisest financially. I love all aspects of the fiber medium but have fallen hard for beading. I'm now a senior citizen and devote my time to making art. I live in Waltham, Massachusetts, where I spend my days beadweaving, exploring the book arts, and writing poetry.

www.kaydolezal.com

"I make some pieces as political commentary and others just for the fun of it, to see if an idea will work in beads."

B

A *Prayer Rug #1*, 2009
66 x 81.3 cm
Glass seed beads, silamide thread;
right angle weave
Photo by Gail Handelmann

B *Hand Grenade*, 2003
10.2 x 5.7 cm
Glass seed beads, silamide thread,
metal ring; right angle weave
Photo by David Caras

WHEN AND HOW DID YOU BEGIN WORKING WITH BEADS?

I started in 1995. I was inspired by an article in *Threads* magazine about making a beaded amulet bag. I'd been exploring the fiber arts, but once I started beading I never went back. I soaked up the work of Virginia Blakelock, Carol Wilcox Wells, and the other bead artists who published books in the 1990s. David Chatt also inspired me.

DESCRIBE YOUR WORK.

I view it as weaving. Calling right angle weave an off-loom weave stitch has real meaning for me. I can construct a piece while sitting on my couch and stitching quietly, but I'm making what I hope is a strong statement with beads, needle, and thread. I alternate between size 8 and size 11 beads. I love the weight that larger beads accumulate as a piece progresses. This literally adds substance to what I'm saying or playing with.

WHAT'S YOUR WORKING PROCESS LIKE? IS THERE MUCH PLANNING INVOLVED?

I do plan. I graph out flat pieces beforehand. For three-dimensional pieces, I may take some time to figure out how to do them, either by experimenting with beads or finding an armature that will work. I make color choices as I go

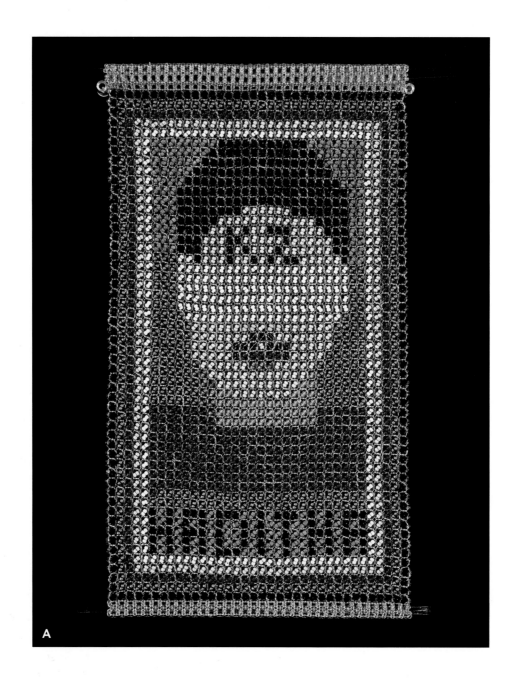

A

B

A *Haditha*, 2005
36.9 x 21.6 cm
Glass seed beads, silamide thread, glass rods; right angle weave
Photo by David Caras

B *From the Barrier Tape Series: Bright Line*, 2005
6.4 x 81.3 cm
Glass seed beads, silamide thread; right angle weave
Photo by David Caras

C *Bubble Wrap—Unpopped*, 2008
Unrolled: 14.6 x 190.5 cm
Glass seed beads, silamide thread; right angle weave
Photo by Gail Handelmann

D *Four from the Pot Holder Series*, 2006
Each: 15.2 x 15.2 cm
Glass seed beads, silamide thread; right angle weave
Photo by David Caras

along. A color may not work. Then I'll have to undo the piece and try something else.

HAS YOUR WORKING PROCESS EVOLVED?
I started out making jewelry and trying various stitches. But, since 2001, I've limited myself to the single-needle right angle weave stitch, because it makes a beautifully fluid flat piece and can be added to so that each side of a flat piece is different or can be built up into three-dimensional structures. Although I love the fluid quality of a single layer of right angle weave, I developed a process whereby I make a grid similar to a needlepoint base and then fill it in with two more layers. This sort of piece can get quite heavy, so it needs to be displayed flat, which has given me the chance to make some oriental-type rugs. This particular process makes it easy to graph letters and allows me to incorporate text into my work.

HOW DOES THE PUBLIC RESPOND TO YOUR WORK?
Some people have trouble believing that there's no fabric holding the work together. And of course, people want to touch the beads. Since that's part of what I love about beads, I usually encourage it.

"You might not think beads could be political, but Kay is making a strong point with her work."

—SUZANNE GOLDEN

douglas w. johnson

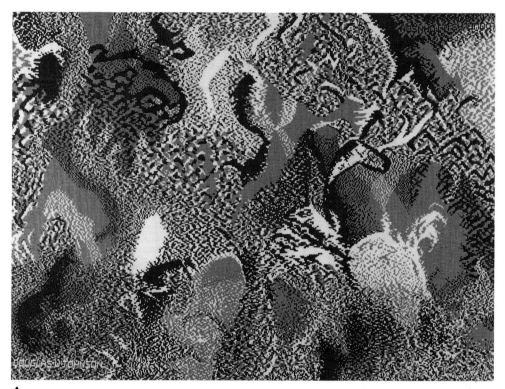

A

Originally from Bristol, Connecticut, I started out as a singer-songwriter. My band, Sweet Potato Pie, toured New England in the 1970s. I became interested in the art of beading during that time. I now have a studio—I call it my Bead Bunker—in Newburyport, Massachusetts, on historic High Street. My looms are there, along with my collection of many thousands of tiny glass beads. I live in Newburyport with my partner, Alda Maria, and have two grown children. Over the past 30 years, I've created more than 200 glass canvases, many of which are now housed in private collections or displayed in corporate lobbies. My pieces have also been featured on HGTV. I think of my work as bead painting.

www.douglaswjohnson.com

"Beading on a loom is a process of unlimited possibilities."

DESCRIBE YOUR WORK. The fine art of beading executed with painstaking joy.

WHAT RESPONSE DO YOU GET TO IT? Quite often, people are amazed at the degree of detail and the sense of illustration that I'm able to achieve through the weaving of beads rather than through painting.

DESCRIBE YOUR WORKING PROCESS. DO YOU WORK FROM PHOTOS OR SKETCHES? I get inspired by scenes I observe on my daily walks—an architectural detail on a historic house, or a field full of wildflowers. Sometimes I'll snap a picture.

B

C

A *Color Wars*, 2010
57.2 x 77.5 cm
Seed beads,
nylon thread
Photo by artist

B *The Mall in the
Fall*, 2006
58.4 x 81.3 cm
Seed beads,
nylon thread
Photo by Matthew F.
Napoleon

C *Plum Island*, 2003
53.3 x 88.9 cm
Seed beads, nylon
thread
Photo by Matthew F.
Napoleon

YOU COULD PAINT OR DRAW THESE SCENES. WHY DO YOU USE BEADS?

When I started beadweaving, it was a hobby. It's now my passion. When I finish a piece, I can't wait to start another one. I've never had the desire to use any other medium. Beading on a loom is what I've loved to do for the past 30 years. A bead artist is who I am.

DO YOU PLAN, OR DO YOU DESIGN AS YOU GO?

Sometimes the process is all about planning, and sometimes it's about letting go and surrendering to pure inspiration. I like to render what I see in my familiar medium and put my spin on it. Over the years, I've collected a palette of more than a thousand bead colors. I've also become more familiar

A

B

> "My favorite is the image of everyone on a cell phone. It's a very contemporary statement. Douglas' detail work is amazing."
>
> —SUZANNE GOLDEN

with my custom looms. Both factors enable me to give more detail to my work and to keep evolving.

WHAT MOTIVATES YOUR WORK?
Challenge inspires me—the challenge of producing fine art through the threading of tiny glass seed beads.

WHAT'S YOUR FAVORITE PART OF WORKING WITH BEADS?
I love weaving tiny glass seed beads into fine-art tapestries—into pieces that interpret what I envision in my mind.

C

A *View from the Pru*,
2007
45.7 x 104.1 cm
Seed beads, nylon thread
Photo by artist

B *View from the Green
Monster*, 2009
76.2 x 88.9 cm
Seed beads, nylon thread
Photo by Matthew F. Napoleon

C *Cocktails, Anyone?*,
2010
40.6 x 68.6 cm
Seed beads, nylon thread
Photo by Matthew F. Napoleon

D *North Shore Marsh*,
2002
50.8 x 88.9 cm
Seed beads, nylon thread
Photo by Matthew F. Napoleon

D

WHEN AND HOW DID YOU BEGIN BEADING?

Lana Pettey, a musician and accomplished beader, introduced me to beading in 1970. I strung beads into necklaces at first but soon learned how to weave them on a loom and—being a guitar player—decided to make a guitar strap. So I built a long loom and wove a strip of beads that could be sewn onto leather. Then I thought it would be nice to get wilder and make a scene out of beads—a house, a barn, even a little village. To create the scenes, I built a loom that could hold four strips in a row, each about 25 beads wide. I wove each strip separately and sewed them together. It wasn't until 1990 that I figured out how to connect the rows on the loom to produce a solid piece. Now I'm making works comprised of up to 300,000 beads.

christine marie noguere

A

I came to the world of beads and jewelry design in a roundabout way. In the 1970s, my brother and I created carved and dyed leatherwork that we sold to many of the day's biggest rock stars. I went on to study cinematography, earning an MFA from the University of South Florida. I spent 13 years in Florida, the Caribbean, and New York working on feature films, commercials, and other projects. In 1994, I moved to the mountains of north Georgia and married my college sweetheart, Phil Pope. We bought some forest acreage in Marble Hill, Georgia, named it Paradise eNow, and camped out for several years while we built a house with our own hands. I studied beading at the Japanese Embroidery Center in Dunwoody, Georgia, and took classes in Japanese bead embroidery from Reiko Matsukawa of Japan. I've since exhibited my work in museums and galleries across the nation.

www.paradise-enow.com

"I create sculptural jewelry and sculptures of jewelry."

B

C

A *Arc to Arcturas (Jewelry for Giants, No. 6)*, 2011
23 x 19 x 15 cm
Japanese glass cylinder and seed beads, cork ball, butyl cord, maple, pearlescent paints; right angle weave, peyote stitch, bent, laminated, painted
Photo by Phil Pope

B *Aurora*, 2005
27.3 x 28 x 1 cm
Japanese glass seed beads, butyl rings; right angle weave, circular brick stitch
Photo by Phil Pope

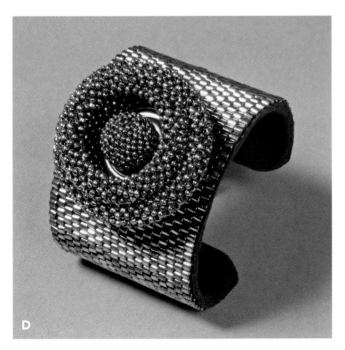

D

C *Olympus Mons*, 2005
7 x 6.4 x 5.1 cm
Japanese glass cylinder and seed beads, 14-karat gold-filled beads, butyl rings, brass, suedelike material; peyote stitch, right angle weave, embellished
Photo by Phil Pope

D *Solar Constant*, 2005
6.7 x 6.4 x 5.1 cm
Japanese glass cylinder and seed beads, hand-made glass disk, cork ball, butyl rings, brass, suedelike material; peyote stitch, right angle weave
Photo by Phil Pope

WHAT DO YOU ENJOY MOST ABOUT WORKING WITH BEADS?
I enjoy the solitude of beading. I live in the middle of a forest in a house that my husband and I built with our own hands. When I'm beading, I can look up from my work, see a deer walk by, watch the birds and squirrels, and remember how lucky I am to be doing what I'm doing.

WHEN AND HOW DID YOU BEGIN BEADING?
Beading had been on my mind for many years, but I always seemed to find other handwork that took precedence over it. In 2002, I finally bought a book about beadweaving and started making jewelry by myself. I then took classes from Virginia Blakelock, Carol Perrenoud, and David Chatt.

HOW DO YOU CHOOSE THE BEADS YOU USE?
I have a definite idea of my color scheme before I begin. I seek out the beads that will realize the mental picture I have of the finished piece. I often use matte beads or a monochromatic palette to emphasize the shape of the piece rather than the beauty of individual beads.

WHAT CAUSED YOU TO START WORKING ON A LARGE SCALE?

My *Jewelry for Giants* series was conceived while I was listening to Wagner's *Ring* cycle. The four operas about gods, giants, and a magic ring conjured up rich images of a mythical world of wonders. I was inspired to adorn Wagner's larger-than-life beings, so my work grew from human-size sculptural jewelry to actual sculptures of jewelry, which are three times as large as life size.

TAKE US THROUGH YOUR WORKING PROCESS.

The designs for my work are completed before I begin beading. I envision the completed piece and try to bring it to life. I make drawings, create armatures—a process that can be as involved as beadweaving—and then bead.

HAS YOUR WORKING PROCESS EVOLVED OVER TIME?

My pieces have gotten larger and now require different materials, so I've had to learn other disciplines like woodworking and silversmithing. I've also had to learn the discipline of patience.

A *Hyakutake (Jewelry for Giants, No. 4)*, 2007
23 x 19 x 15 cm
Japanese glass cylinder and seed beads, Czech fire-polished beads, wooden cube, butyl cord, maple, pearlescent paints; right angle weave, peyote, embellished, bent, laminated, painted
Photo by Phil Pope

B *Astraea*, 2009
9 x 7 x 4.8 cm
Crystal cube and round beads, Japanese glass seed beads, cork ball, butyl ring, sterling silver sheet, round and square sterling silver wire; square stitch, right angle weave, fabricated
Photo by Phil Pope

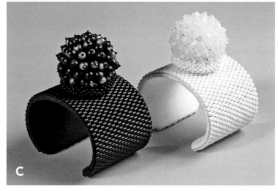

C *Mutual Attraction*, 2004
Each: 8.3 x 6.4 x 5.1 cm
Japanese glass cylinder and seed beads, Czech beads, hex beads, wooden beads, Teflon and butyl rings, brass, suedelike material; peyote stitch, right angle weave, embellished
Photo by Phil Pope

D *Titania (Jewelry for Giants, No. 5)*, 2007
23 x 19 x 15 cm
Japanese glass cylinder and seed beads, cork ball, butyl cord, maple, pearlescent paints; right angle weave, peyote stitch, bent, laminated, painted
Photo by Phil Pope

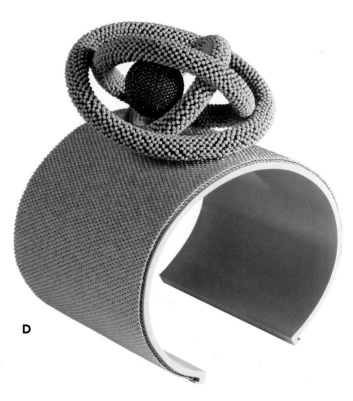

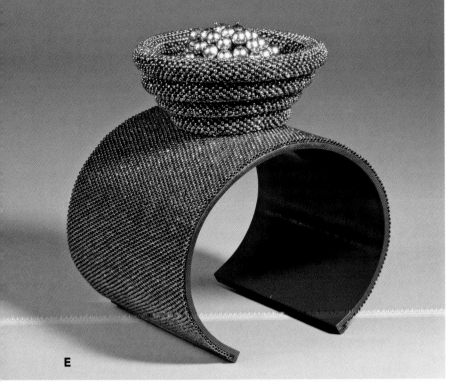

E

F

G

A piece of jewelry may take a few weeks to complete, whereas a sculpture requires several months of work.

WHAT INSPIRES YOUR WORK?
One of the things that inspires me is astronomy, which is often reflected in the titles of my work. I love astronomical photographs, especially the ones sent back from the Cassini spacecraft, which has been photographing Saturn and its moons since 2004.

"I was immediately drawn to Christine's work because of its elegant lines and understated elegance."

—SUZANNE GOLDEN

E *Alma Venus (Jewelry for Giants, No. 1)*, 2006
22 x 19 x 15 cm
Japanese glass cylinder and seed beads, Japanese acrylic beads, wooden ball, butyl cord, maple, pearlescent paints; right angle weave, peyote stitch, embellished, bent, laminated, painted
Photo by Phil Pope

F *Antares*, 2008
9.5 x 6.4 x 5.1 cm
Japanese glass cylinder and seed beads, Czech beads, sterling silver pins, cork ball, butyl rings, brass, suedelike material; right angle weave, peyote stitch
Photo by Phil Pope

G *Tea at the Palaz of Hoon*, 2007
23.5 x 21.6 x 11.4 cm
Japanese glass seed beads, aluminum, steel, butyl cord, cork ball, oak, pearlescent paints; right angle weave, circular brick stitch, peyote stitch, fabricated
Photo by Phil Pope

leslie b. grigsby

I live in Chadds Ford, Pennsylvania. In addition to making art as a bead-work sculptor, I serve as senior curator of ceramics and glass at the Winter-thur Museum in Winter-thur, Delaware. Since 2006, my work has often involved collaboration with my husband, Lind-say, and been displayed in several galleries, includ-ing the Snyderman-Works Galleries in Philadelphia. It has also been shown in New York and Chicago at the Annual International Exposition of Sculpture Objects & Functional Art (SOFA). My pieces are in-cluded in the collections of the National Aeronautics and Space Administra-tion and the Kamm Teapot Foundation, as well as in several private collections.

lbgrigsbybeadwork.
wordpress.com

A *Egyptian Teapot*, 2012
43.2 x 42.5 x 33 cm
Glass and metal seed and
cylinder beads, wood,
thread, paint; peyote,
square, and ladder stitch
Courtesy of the Kamm Teapot
Foundation
Photos by artist

B *Teapot: If You Drink Any More Tea, You'll Turn into a Fish!*, 2009
29.2 x 40.6 x 21.6 cm
Wood and glass seed beads, wood, thread, paint
Courtesy of the Kamm Teapot Foundation
Photos by artist

WHAT'S YOUR FAVORITE PART OF WORKING WITH BEADS?
Working with beads, especially seed beads, which require quite a bit of time and patience when applied to large surfaces, is very calming. The freedom from elaborate tools, the flexibility of the medium, and the comparatively low cost of the materials also are pluses.

HOW DO YOU CHOOSE YOUR IMAGERY AND THE TYPES OF PIECES YOU BEAD?
Many of my images have followed me throughout my life and reflect interests shared by my parents, brothers, and sister since childhood. The images and concepts grow from our fascinations with science, music, history, and travel. A few of my sculptures—such as *The Four Elements* series— were created as sets, reflecting themes that have been portrayed in art for centuries.

"The colors and textures of the world are irresistible to me. They permeate my work."

HOW WOULD YOU DESCRIBE YOUR WORK?

It's a vehicle that allows me to put into concrete, three-dimensional form concepts that continually float in and out of my dreams. I use off-loom beadweaving techniques to create sheaths of imagery superimposed over contrasting sculptural forms. The process is very rewarding.

TELL US A LITTLE ABOUT YOUR WORKING PROCESS.

For many projects, my work usually begins as a series of rough sketches, which I often discuss with my husband, Lindsay, who plays a major role in creating the wooden cores of some of my sculptures. I typically make measured drawings for such cores. In contrast, the beadwork portion of my pieces continually evolves. It begins as a general concept that soon gets a mind of its own and takes me along with it.

A

B

C

A *Raygun No. 3*, 2009
21 cm long
Glass and metal seed beads, wood;
peyote and square stitch
Private collection
Photo by artist

B From the *Four Elements
Series: Earth: The Root of
All Good*, 2010
27.3 x 20.3 cm
Glass seed beads, thread,
wood, paint; peyote stitch
Photo by artist

C From the *Four Elements
Series: Water: Are You the
Island or the Avenue?*, 2010
21.6 x 19.1 cm
Glass seed beads, thread, wood,
paint; square stitch
Photo by artist

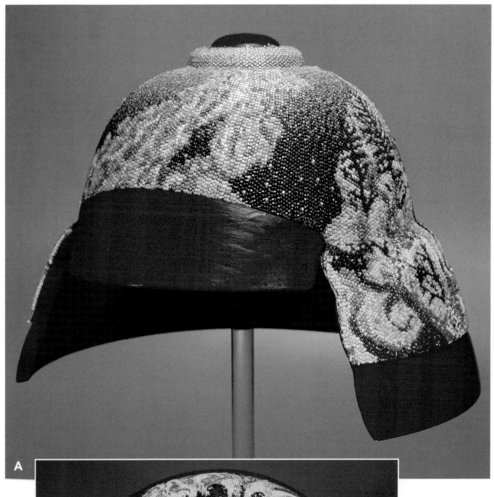

A From the *Four Elements Series:*
Fire: Destruction or Rebirth?, 2010
22.2 x 30.5 cm
Glass seed beads, thread, wood, paint;
peyote stitch
Photos by artist

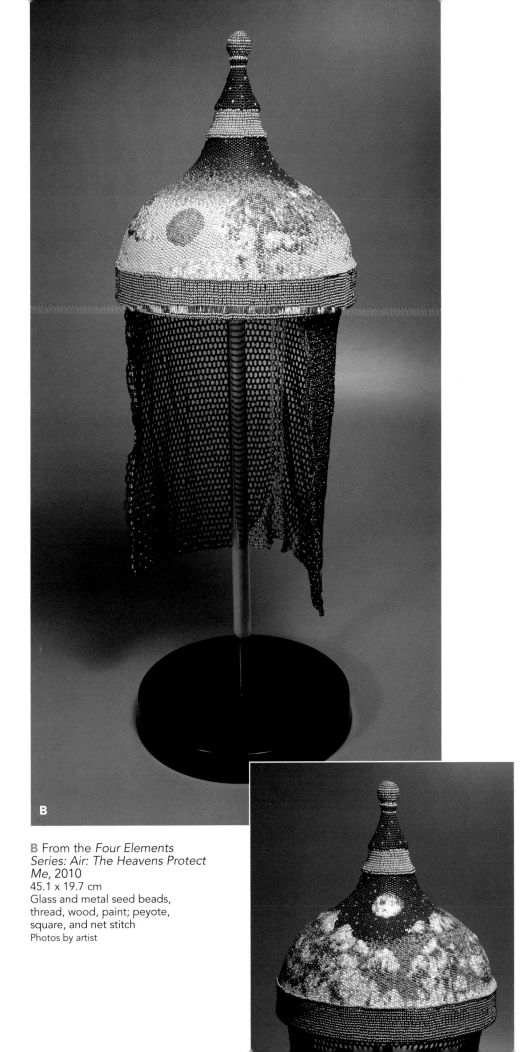

B From the *Four Elements Series: Air: The Heavens Protect Me*, 2010
45.1 x 19.7 cm
Glass and metal seed beads, thread, wood, paint; peyote, square, and net stitch
Photos by artist

HOW DO YOU CHOOSE THE BEADS YOU USE?

I usually work with a limited size range of seed beads (15/0 to 6/0, with 11/0 to 12/0 being the most typical) and have a good sense of the primary ranges of colors and shading I'll need. For subtle transitions, I may purchase smaller quantities of beads as the project progresses. I prefer to view beads in person instead of online, because I don't trust the colors I see on the computer screen.

HOW DO PEOPLE REACT TO YOUR WORK?

"Are you crazy?" is the most common response, especially in regard to my larger projects, which can take more than a year to complete.

"Leslie's elegant and mystical beaded helmets leave you imagining the types of warriors who might have worn these inventive headdresses in days gone by—or in days to come."

—SUZANNE GOLDEN

uliana volkhovskaya

I was born in Russia, but when I was a child, my family moved to Ukraine, to the city of Dnepropetrovsk, where I still live. I attended an art school for youth and then college, where my major had nothing to do with being creative. I'm now a housewife and mother, and beading has become a very important part of my life. My family supports me, and this is very important. My husband and my daughter are always glad to see my work. They inspire me and push me forward!

www.artbiser.dp.ua

A *The Baggage Maroussia*, 2011
15 cm tall
Seed beads, glass beads, thread;
peyote stitch, brick stitch
Photos by artist

"Each piece brings new challenges—new stitches and techniques."

B

C

B *What Baby Do You Want—a Girl or a Boy?*, 2011
15 cm tall
Seed beads, glass beads, thread, wire;
peyote stitch, right angle weave, fringed
Photo by artist

C *Little Raccoon*, 2012
13 cm tall
Seed beads, glass beads, thread; peyote
stitch, right angle weave, fringed
Photos by artist

HOW DID YOU GET INTO BEADING?
I'm a self-taught beadweaver. I've never taken a class. I started beading after my daughter brought home a gift made by a friend—a trinket with a beaded crocodile. I became interested in how the critter was made. I found an online forum for bead lovers and began learning different bead techniques. I found that I liked the peyote stitch best of all. The beads are tight, the thread is almost invisible, and the beaded surface is fairly solid and flexible. I eventually learned how to change the shape of the beaded canvas and started making mini sculptures.

YOUR CONSTRUCTION METHODS ARE QUITE SOPHISTICATED. ARE YOUR FIGURES STUFFED OR EMPTY? DO THEIR LIMBS MOVE?
The figures I create don't have "skeletons" or frames. Some of them are static. With these figures, I focus on tiny details that

A *Mouse King*, 2010
16 cm tall
Seed beads, glass beads, crystal
elements, thread; peyote stitch,
herringbone stitch, right angle
weave, hand woven
Photos by artist

B *The Cow Murka*, 2011
14 cm tall
Seed beads, glass beads, thread;
peyote stitch
Photos by artist

will make viewers pay attention to them and wonder about them. Most of the figures I make are dynamic, with movable limbs. I stuff these figures with synthetic materials that make them light, soft, and springy.

WHAT INSPIRES THE FIGURES?

I'm inspired by cartoons, funny pictures, scenes from daily life. Art is a very important source of inspiration. There are a lot of eye-catching beadworks out there that amaze me. Interesting color combinations and unusual shapes and designs also inspire me.

WHAT RESPONSES DO THEY GET?

I receive a lot of e-mails with thanks for the smiles and happiness my work brings. Adults become children when they play with my pieces. Mischief and delight appear in their eyes!

A *Clowns*, 2011
15 cm tall
Seed beads, glass beads,
thread; peyote stitch
Photos by artist

B *Royal Jester*, 2011
22 cm tall
Seed beads, glass beads,
crystal elements, wire,
thread; peyote stitch
Photos by artist

B

DO YOU DO MUCH PLANNING TO CREATE YOUR FIGURES?

I don't plan the result in advance. My work starts with a question: "What will happen if… ?" My process consists of a few steps: thinking about ideas, defining the elements of a composition, selecting materials, weaving, putting elements together, and evaluating the results. Each stage is interesting in its own way. When I look at a finished piece, I might feel admiration, but just for a few seconds. Then I move on!

"I am smitten with Uliana's pieces. They are utterly charming and make me smile. And her workmanship is flawless."

—SUZANNE GOLDEN

eva maria keiser

I was born in Vienna, Austria, but now call Boise, Idaho, home. I started beading in 2000. I went from application software education to working as an artist. Over time, my needlework has transitioned into three-dimensional narratives in which beads serve as building blocks. My passion is architecting structural beadworks that have opulent color schemes, elegant shapes, and layers of detail. Each of my pieces emerges organically and intuitively, one bead at a time. When I'm not beading, I'm sleeping!

www.keiserdesigns.com

A & B *Double-Decker Ring Box*, 2012
10 x 6 x 6 cm
Crystals, cylinder beads, seed beads, fire-polished beads, leather; peyote stitch, right angle weave
Photos by artist

"My structural beadworks are inspired by the transition of light, the play of color, and form."

WHAT'S YOUR FAVORITE PART OF WORKING WITH BEADS?

Beads are just the means to a realized expression. My work isn't about the medium—it's about integrity of design. However, I do appreciate the dimensional and light transitional qualities of beads.

DESCRIBE YOUR WORK.

My pieces are "made-only-once" architected designs with layers of detail, surprising interiors, and unique colors and shapes.

HOW DO YOU WORK? DO YOU PLAN MUCH?

The process is always the same: thread up one or two needles, dip into a bead mixture, and allow a design to emerge. A documented digital photo journal is the extent of my sketchbook. Revisiting my extensive collection of explored elements inspires me. These images are often integrated into new work.

C *Celeste*, 2011
18 x 10 x 5.5 cm
Cylinder beads, bugle beads, seed beads, fire-polished beads, bicones, rivolis, montées; peyote stitch, herringbone stitch, netting, right angle weave
Photos by artist

D *T-Hex (Tetrakis-Hexahedron)*, 2011
15.2 x 15.2 x 15.2 cm
Cylinder beads, bugle beads, seed beads, fire-polished beads; peyote stitch
Photo by artist

HAS THIS EVOLVED OVER TIME?

My working process has not changed at all. What has changed is my ability to trust and surrender to the artistic process.

ARE YOUR VESSELS SUPPORTED BY ARMATURES OR PURCHASED FORMS?

All of my vessel designs are self-supported by multiple beadworked layers that are further sometimes embellished or bead embroidered. Unsupported hollow structures such as eggs, beaded beads, or spheres are fiber-filled.

YOUR BRACELETS HAVE AN INTERIOR PATTERN THAT'S DIFFERENT FROM THE PATTERN ON THE EXTERIOR. YET THE INTERIOR DOESN'T SHOW WHEN THE BRACELETS ARE WORN. WHY DO YOU DESIGN IN THIS MANNER?

Each of my pieces is designed as an object of art and comprised of multiple layers. The interiors are designed to be unique. A piece may fit the wrist and be considered a bracelet, but it isn't designed as such. The function is subjective. For example, the smaller ring elements I create may be

A *Bugle Star Cluster*, 2010
10.5 x 10.5 x 10.5 cm
Seed beads, cylinder beads, copper metal beads, bugle beads, copper jump rings; peyote stitch, herringbone stitch
Photo by artist

B *Turquoise Dance*, 2009
20.5 x 10 x 8.5 cm
Seed beads, cylinder beads, bugle beads, palladium beads, sterling silver beads, crystals and glass pearls, turquoise round beads; peyote stitch, herringbone stitch, right angle weave, bead embroidery
Photos by artist

C *Chess King Vessel,* 2012
20 x 13 x 6.5 cm
Cylinder beads, bugle beads, seed beads, fire-polished beads, round jet beads, montées, fringe; peyote stitch, herringbone stitch, netting, right angle weave
Photos by artist

perceived as pendants or napkin rings. Larger rings can be used to embellish vases or candles and can serve as curtain tiebacks. Combinations of ring sizes form jewelry elements, items of containment, and/or sculptures. The possibilities are endless.

WHAT RESPONSES DO YOU GET TO YOUR WORK?
Frequent responses include: incredible detail, unique design, opulent color, marvelous modulation, excellent structural composition.

D *Celebrate,* 2010
21 x 10 x 8.5 cm
Seed beads, cylinder beads, bugle beads, fire-polished beads, silver beads, fringe, crystals and rivoli beads; peyote stitch, herringbone stitch, brick stitch, netting, right angle weave
Photo by artist

E *Spring Splash,* 2010
25 x 8.9 x 8 cm
Seed beads, cylinder beads, silver beads, fire-polished jet beads, jet focal bead, copper metal beads, vintage jet button, crystals, turquoise beads; peyote stitch, brick stitch, herringbone stitch, netting, right angle weave
Photo by artist

"Eva Maria's work never fails to surprise me. I'm impressed with the various techniques used and delight in the finished results."
—SUZANNE GOLDEN

arianne van der gaag

I attended art school in Utrecht, Netherlands. The jewelry and objects I design reflect my love for the materials I work with. In addition to creating jewelry, I frequently serve as a curator and programmer. My work has been exhibited in several galleries and purchased by museums and private collectors. I now live in Rotterdam, where I have my own studio space in an old school building.

www.ariannevandergaag.nl

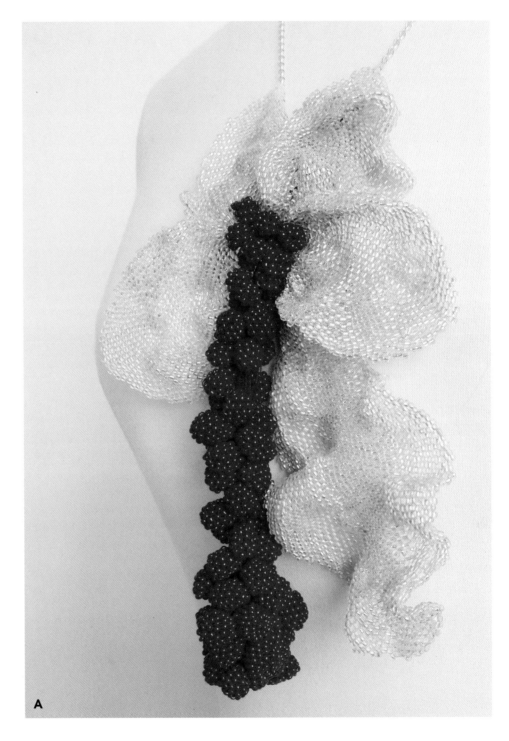

A

"I use beads to create my own language."

B

A Untitled, 2011
42 x 13 x 4 cm
Antique beads, glass
beads; strung
Photo by artist

B Untitled, 2010
90 x 50 x 30 cm
Glass beads, wood; strung
Photos by Rens Horn

CAN YOU TALK A BIT ABOUT YOUR AESTHETIC CHOICES?

My work has to answer a notion of intrinsic value. It's all about passion, inspiration, and endurance and expresses sentiments that I can't put into words. It reflects a permanent state of searching.

HOW DO YOU DESCRIBE YOUR WORK?

An important theme is the repetition of similar elements that together form a larger, integrated whole. Organic shapes develop from the inside out. Small details create a unified work. The materials I use make the work look fragile, lovely, delicate, and sometimes abstract. There's a darkness behind the delicate exterior. Growth and decay are both present, representing the core of life. I use mostly small beads because they let me say what I'm trying to say better than larger beads do.

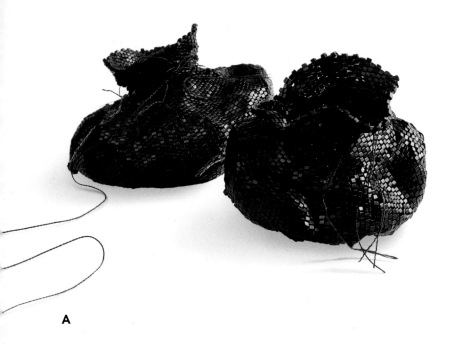

A

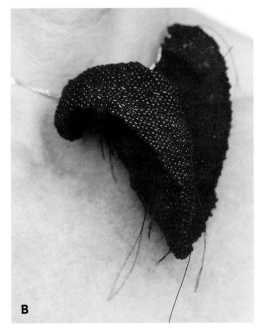

B

C

D

A Untitled, 2010
7 x 9 x 12 cm
Glass beads; strung
Photo by Rens Horn

B Untitled, 2007
21 x 13 x 4.5 cm
Glass beads, silver; strung
Photo by Rens Horn

C Untitled, 2008
55 x 13 x 2.5 cm
Glass beads; strung
Photo by Rens Horn

D Untitled, 2007
19 x 16 x 2.5 cm
Antique beads; strung
Photo by Rens Horn

E Untitled, 2005
21 x 18 x 0.5 cm
Coral; strung
Photo by Rens Horn

F Untitled, 2006
20 x 15.5 x 2 cm
Antique beads; strung
Photo by Rens Horn

E

F

I'm always looking for materials and techniques that support the content of my art. It's a process of continuous growth. I want to be able to express myself better using the tools at hand.

WHAT'S YOUR FAVORITE PART OF WORKING WITH BEADS?

Actually making a piece—putting it together—is the best. Making is thinking. Each of my actions has a consequence for the final form. When I've finished a piece, I'm frequently surprised. The result is often something I never imagined.

WHEN DID YOU BEGIN BEADING?

I've long had a private fascination with beads. When I was in school, I began to collect beads, but I didn't know how to work with them without seeming old-fashioned. A few years later, I found a little book about beading and that got me started. I haven't stopped! I love the fact that the essence of the bead is a little hole and that the emptiness—the hole—is what makes the bead complete.

"I like the contrast between the hardness and the softness of Arianne's work. I find it to be very organic."

—SUZANNE GOLDEN

axel russmeyer

Axel Russmeyer was born in 1964 in Bad Oldesloe, Germany. After setting up his own studio and gallery in Hamburg in the late '80s, he worked as a freelance designer and artist. In 1993 he received a degree in communication design. Since then, he has shown at galleries in both the United States and Europe. Russmeyer's jewelry collection has been found at prestigious shops and museums such as MOMA Design Store, Barney's New York, Takashimaya, and currently at Kentshire, Bergdorf Goodman, and Ted Muehling in New York. Examples of his work are in the permanent collection of the Metropolitan Museum of Art in New York, the Mint Museum in Charlotte, the Victoria and Albert Museum in London, and the Museum für Kunst und Gewerbe in Hamburg.

Blues!, 2006
Each beaded bead:
3.1 cm in diameter
Vintage and contemporary glass and metal seed beads, wood, thread, paint
Photo by Geoff Onyett

"Beads themselves are my source of inspiration. They invite me to thread the needle."

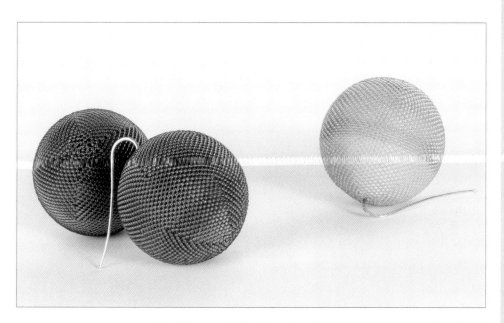

Ping Pong, 2007
Each: 4.8 cm in diameter
Japanese glass seed beads, thread,
paint, Ping-Pong balls, 18-karat gold
Photos by Geoff Onyett

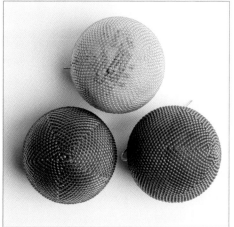

Antique Pigeon Blue, 2004
Beaded bead: 2.3 cm in diameter
Antique flat doughnut-shaped
glass beads, wood, thread
Photos by Geoff Onyett

My life is a story of collecting, creating, and presenting. Beads have been a part of my artistic activities for as long as I can remember—from early childhood, when they were components of craft projects, to my teenage years, when I was captivated by old varieties of them while hunting for treasures at flea markets. The methods I have used to incorporate beads into my artistic oeuvre are driven by their innate qualities. I was never formally taught any beading techniques. I have moved through many stages of creativity with beads, receptive to all that was in front of my eyes.

The variety of beads is utterly infinite—in size, texture, refraction, color, and so on. I feel that the way I use them—even though I'm always making spheres—must be as far-reaching as possible, to enhance their wonderful, inherent qualities. That's why I only use one kind of bead for each individual sphere. On the other hand, I might change the thread color one or more times within an individual bead.

I made my first beaded beads in the late '80s and I haven't changed the innate shape of my work—beaded and sequined beads—since then.

"Axel's beaded bead necklaces transcend the usual and become art to wear. Nobody does it better!"

—SUZANNE GOLDEN

Tin Metal Garden Sphere, 2005
42 cm in diameter
Sheet-metal baking forms,
stainless steel ball, hemp rope,
glass seed beads, thread, wood
Photos by Geoff Onyett

Variations of Gray and Grey, 1999
Largest beaded bead: 4.1 cm in diameter
Wooden core, antique and
contemporary glass and metal beads,
freshwater pearls, silk ribbon, sterling
silver seals; strung, knotted
Photos by Geoff Onyett

Times Two, 2005
Largest beaded bead: 2.8 cm in diameter
Glass seed beads, miracle beads, crystal beads, various threads, wood, acrylic glass, ribbon, 18-karat gold clasps, paint; beaded, knotted
Photo by Geoff Onyett

Furry Fur, 2000
Each beaded bead: 2.7 cm in diameter
Glass beads, chenille yarns, seed beads, wood, thread
Photo by Geoff Onyett

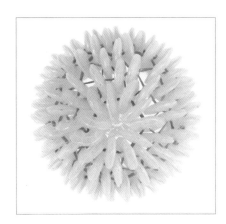

Gold and Honey Candy, 2003
Beaded beads: 4.5 x 8 x 12 cm
Plastic, resin, miracle beads, fiber-optic
beads, holographic glitter, various
threads, elastic cord, wood
Photo by Geoff Onyett

Two at a Time, 2004
Sequined bead: 2 cm
in diameter
Vintage plastic cupped
sequins, acrylic glass
beads, thread
Photos by Geoff Onyett

Golden Green, 2005
Sequined bead: 2.5 cm
in diameter
Plastic sequins, thread, wood
Photo by Geoff Onyett

Shiny Pink!, 2004
Sequined bead: 4.5 cm
in diameter
Thin antique colored metal
sequins, thread, wood
Photos by Geoff Onyett

sherry markovitz

I was born in Chicago but have lived in Seattle since 1971. I hold a BA from the University of Wisconsin and an MFA from the University of Washington. I've shown my work nationally and internationally since 1979. My husband is a sculptor, and we have a 24-year-old son who seems destined to be an artist. We built our home-studio in Seattle in 1980. My workspace is beautiful, with lots of good light. It's truly my sanctuary.

A

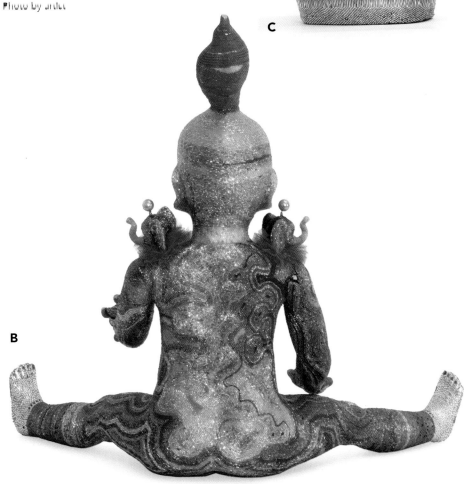

A & B *Crowning*, 2009
66 x 79 x 39 cm
Papier-mâché, glue, seed beads, mixed media
Courtesy of the Lora Schlesinger Gallery
Courtesy of the Greg Kucera Gallery
Photos by artist

C *Mummy Bear*, 2010
49 x 36 x 26 cm
Papier-mâché, thread, seed beads
Private collection
Photo by artist

C

B

"I seem to have always known about beads."

WHAT IS YOUR WORK ABOUT?

My work is about animating the inanimate. It's about blending observations and dreamlike sensations into forms using color, light, transparency, and opacity.

WHEN AND HOW DID YOU BEGIN WORKING WITH BEADS?

I started studying beads at the age of nine. During my high school and college years, I saw exhibits of Native American and aboriginal art in Chicago that inspired me. But it took me many years—after getting an MA in printmaking, doing photography, and making paintings that had beaded edges—to take beads as my main medium. I first used them seriously in 1980. In 1982, I presented my first beaded deer head.

WHAT ARE YOUR FAVORITE ASPECTS OF WORKING WITH BEADS?

I love the meditative quality of the process. And the color.

WHAT LED TO YOUR PARTICULAR STYLE AND METHOD?

I began using beads to hem large, loose paintings. I then went to painted, cutout images, then to three-dimensional forms, which I was still painting. One day, I was feeling exhausted by the work of combining painted images with beads. I was frustrated, so I just stopped thinking and let the beads take over. I ended up beading the whole form.

CAN YOU TELL US ABOUT YOUR PROCESS?

I usually come up with an idea, make a form or painting, and then look at it for a long time. Sometimes I do sketches. I just keep on going and thinking about the form, sometimes painting or drawing on it.

HOW DO YOU CHOOSE BEADS?

My choices depend on the needs of each project. I consider color, size, type—faceted or opaque—etc.

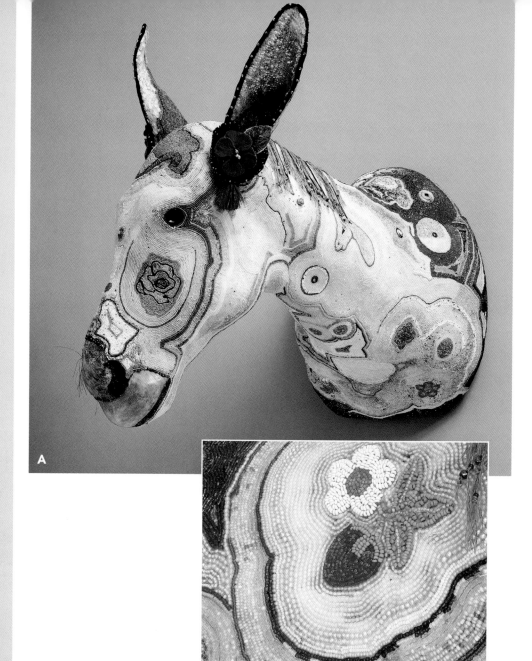

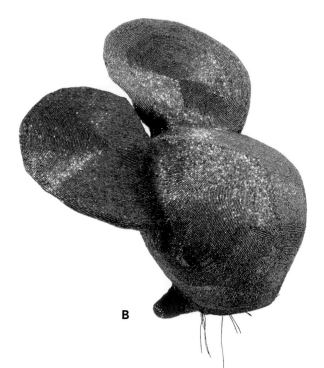

A *My Mule*, 2006
39 x 46 x 86 cm
Papier-mâché, seed beads, thread, glue, mixed media
Private collection
Photo by artist

B *Green Mouse*, 2010
46 x 51 x 51 cm
Papier-mâché, glue, seed beads
Courtesy of the Greg Kucera Gallery
Photo by artist

WHERE DO YOU FIND INSPIRATION?
I'm an insatiable searcher. I look at everything. In particular, I love global forms that utilize beads. I love Native American beadwork, painting, minimalist sculpture, and human and animal facial expressions.

DOES ANYTHING ELSE INFORM YOUR CREATIVE PROCESS?
It's important to me to keep up a practice in both painting and sculpture. For me, that's the conversation I maintain with my work.

C *Shimmer*, 2007
161.3 x 90.4 x 83.8 cm
Sequins, beads, felt, velvet, steel
Courtesy of the Greg Kucera Gallery
Photo by artist

D *Black Sheep*, 2010
55.9 x 43.2 x 43.2 cm
Papier-mâché, thread, wire, glue, beads, mixed media
Private collection
Photos by artist

"I'm very intrigued by the symbolism in Sherry's pieces."

—SUZANNE GOLDEN

patricia kraemer

My home is located on 75 acres of rolling hills in southeast Minnesota, on a bluff overlooking the Zumbro River and the village of Zumbro Falls. My studio is on the third floor, above the treetops, with a wonderful view of hills, farmland, river, and, of course, birds. Retired after 32 years of teaching art at Rochester Community and Technical College in Rochester, Minnesota, I happily spend my time working with beads, striving for a harmonious combination of technique and content in my work.

www.patkraemer.com

A

"Beads have it all—the power of light, color, spirit, and a connection to other cultures."

B

C

A *Hummingbird and Barbed Wire*, 2010
66 x 8 x 2 cm
Seed beads; right angle weave, peyote stitch, fringe
Photo by Hugh Kraemer

B *Lovey-Dovey Purse*, 2006
30.5 x 20.3 x 10.2 cm
Glass, vintage Lucite, and wooden beads; bead embroidery
Photo by Hugh Kraemer

D

C *American Traveler WisSota (Wisconsin/Minnesota) Marsh Ducks (Dabblers): Male*, 2007
35.6 x 20.3 x 15.2 cm
Glass beads, vintage beads, semiprecious gems, natural objects, sequins, charms; peyote stitch, brick stitch, square stitch, right angle weave, herringbone stitch, fringe, roping, bead embroidery, bead mosaic
Photo by Hugh Kraemer

D *Mourning Birds*, 2010
Each approximately:
7.6 x 10.2 x 15.2 cm
Beads, charms; various stitches
Photo by Hugh Kraemer

WHEN AND HOW DID YOU BEGIN MAKING THINGS WITH BEADS?
Handwork has always been part of my life. As a child, I spent hours making clothes for my Madame Alexander dolls. I knitted, quilted, embroidered, and took up weaving, spinning, and felting. I love jewelry and became a serious beader in 1994.

HOW WOULD YOU DESCRIBE YOUR WORK?
As an artist I seek to document life with a combination of conflicting ideas and materials. A hummingbird, the most fragile and innocent of birds, is tangled in a brutal web of barbed wire and cannot escape. It is a contrast that reads well for our fragile environment, unemployment, declining health, or whatever injustice the viewer must endure.

WHAT'S YOUR WORKING PROCESS LIKE?
My ideas take time to develop. I enjoy making things, solving problems, and handling the materials while working. Beads have a strong voice, and it takes patience to let that voice come through. Even though I aspire to a high level of craftsmanship in my work, I like to take the time to let the materials guide me.

A *Hacienda Mosaico Parrot,* 2006
29 x 11 x 9 cm
Old buttons, shells; bead embroidery
Photos by Hugh Kraemer

B *WisSota (Wisconsin Minnesota) Sand Hill Cranes: Male (Red); Female (Blue),* 2007
Male: 76.2 x 35.6 x 15.2 cm; female: 66 x 35.6 x 15.2 cm
Glass beads, vintage beads, semiprecious gems, natural objects, sequins, charms; peyote stitch, brick stitch, square stitch, right angle weave, herringbone stitch, fringe, roping, bead embroidery, bead mosaic
Photos by Hugh Kraemer

C

C *Flicker: Fire Mountain Lovebird*, 2007
29 x 11 x 12 cm
Glass seed beads, disks, drops, and rings; bead embroidery
Photo by Hugh Kraemer

D *American Traveler WisSota (Wisconsin/Minnesota) Marsh Ducks (Dabblers): Female*, 2007
35.6 x 20.3 x 15.2 cm
Glass beads, vintage beads, semiprecious gems, natural objects, sequins, charms; peyote stitch, brick stitch, square stitch, right angle weave, herringbone stitch, fringe, roping, bead embroidery, bead mosaic
Photos by Hugh Kraemer

D

WHAT INSPIRES THE WORK?

My work is about ideas. The birds are part of a bead-embellished series of life-sized migratory birds and waterfowl. As an artist, I'm fascinated by the freedom birds have to travel thousands of miles every year. They cross state lines without licenses, enter countries without passports. Look close— My birds carry souvenirs (special beads and charms) as proof of their travels.

WHAT'S YOUR FAVORITE PART OF WORKING WITH BEADS?

I love holding beads in my hands as I work. Their beauty is enchanting. They have the power of light, color, texture, and shape and are a wonderful time tunnel to other cultures and traditions.

DO YOU HAVE ANY ADVICE FOR OTHER ARTISTS?

Don't make "stuff"; make a statement. And be patient. Let the beads show you what to do and which direction to take.

"The shimmery nature of the beads and the kinetic quality of the charms make them perfect embellishments for sculptures of birds. Patricia has chosen the ideal media."

—SUZANNE GOLDEN

christy puetz

I've been creating fiber art and beaded sculptural objects for more than 20 years. I hold a BFA from the University of North Dakota. My artwork has been exhibited around the country and published in numerous books. Phoenix, Arizona, is home for me, and I'm very involved in the art community there. I currently work with Beads of Courage, a nonprofit organization that creates arts-in-medicine programming for children coping with cancer and other serious illnesses. I recently coauthored and illustrated a children's book about bead history, world cultures, and tolerance. I love to work in the yard, research new projects, ride motorcycles—and vacuum.

www.xtyart.com

A *Seeking*, 2012
21 x 58 x 15 cm
Seed beads, cloth, thread, foam, silk pins
Photos by Dave Saker

"I want my work to have an element of mystery about it and be open to interpretation."

B

B *Guilt and Shame Mask*, 2009
27 x 20 x 21 cm
Felt, glass beads, silamide thread;
peyote stitch, bead embroidery
Photo by Dave Saker

C *Minky*, 2011
33 x 15 x 12 cm
Seed beads, foam, cloth, thread;
peyote stitch, bead embroidery
Photos by Dave Saker

C

WHAT'S YOUR FAVORITE ASPECT OF BEADING?

I love that I can change the feel of a piece through the sheen or the size of a bead. I enjoy the challenge and versatility of sizes to do large and small pieces. Because of the nature of the techniques I use, I can get lost in the process and create a focus or a way to work through an idea.

WHEN AND HOW DID YOU START?

I bought a few hanks of seed beads while on a road trip with my mother. I saw them and thought they were beautiful. I didn't know what I would do with them—I didn't know how to bead at the time—but I had to have them. When I got home, I hung them on the wall so that I could look at them. I eventually decided to sew them onto a cloth figure that I'd created. The rest is history. I started to seriously work with beads around 1989.

WHAT IS YOUR WORK ABOUT? WHAT IDEAS ARE YOU EXPLORING?

My past work focused on personalized figures and beaded "false skins" depicting my research on disease, historical events, personality quirks, and mythology. The figures feature exaggerated body parts and poses, and many of them have a comic-book feel. I view them as three-dimensional action figures from different experiences in my life.

My most recent series is titled *Lost Forest*. I used the creatures in this series to explore the emotional toll that physical distance can have on a relationship between two people and the feelings of vulnerability that can result. Many of the creatures have their throats accentuated with beads and sequins to emphasize the sensuality and vulnerability of that part of the body. None of the creatures has eyes. They hold poses that make them appear to be frozen in time, waiting for onlookers to exit so they can secretly move around in the shadows.

I think that I try to depict emotions as physical things that can be touched. When I'm working on a new series, I always have a meaning in mind, but I've found that the depth of a piece's meaning comes out much later, as time goes on. I believe that the subconscious plays a huge role in how my art comes to fruition. I try not to question why I make certain choices. Sometimes I surprise myself.

A

B

C

A *Ruby Throated*, 2011
50 x 42 x 41 cm
Seed beads, foam, sequins, silk rods, silk pins, cloth, silamide thread; bead embroidery, other techniques
Photo by Dave Saker

B *Curious Chuck*, 2011
25 x 10 x 16 cm
Seed beads, cloth, foam, silk pins, silamide thread; peyote stitch, bead embroidery
Photo by Dave Saker

C *Cuca*, 2011
55 x 30 x 25 cm
Seed beads, cloth, silk pins, sequins, shell, foam, glass beads; bead embroidery
Photo by Dave Saker

D *Nigel*, 2009
23 x 35 x 14 cm
Seed beads, cloth, polyester fiberfill,
stone, metal, silamide thread; bead
embroidery
Photo by Dave Saker

E *Namahage*, 2011
19 x 38 x 15 cm
Seed beads, cloth, foam, silamide
thread; peyote stitch, bead embroidery
Photos by Dave Saker

HOW DO YOU DESIGN A PIECE?

I usually get an image in my head and then roll with it. A piece always has the opportunity to change and transform as I work on it, but I usually have it mapped out in my head before I start. I do enjoy the happy accidents that happen along the way, when I try something just for kicks and it ends up being the best part of a piece or inspiring a whole new series.

WHAT RESPONSES DO YOU GET FROM PEOPLE?

Amazement and disbelief. I get lots of questions about the amount of time involved in making a piece, as well as comments on how unique the work is. Viewers are often fascinated by the fact that when they get up close to a piece, it's covered with beads. They feel a deep need to touch them.

HOW DO YOU CHOOSE THE BEADS YOU USE?

Choosing beads for a piece is like going on a treasure hunt with a specific map. I go into my studio and start digging through drawers of beads. I pull out the main beads I need and put them in a big plastic storage bag. The drawers are labeled by color themes: blue/green, red/pink/purple, yellow/brown, black/orange. I like to dig and rediscover beads I bought a long time ago.

"Christy is fearless in her exploration of the subconscious. She mines the forest of our minds to invent creatures of the forest that seem at once vulnerable and mysterious."

—SUZANNE GOLDEN

yael krakowski

I was born in Tiberias, Israel. A graduate of the Bezalel Academy of Art and Design in Jerusalem, I have pieces in the permanent collections of the Montreal Museum of Fine Arts and the Cooper-Hewitt, National Design Museum. In 2003, I left Israel for Canada in search of peace, quiet, and space. I now live in the boonies of Vernon, British Columbia, with my husband and dog. We're surrounded by nature, which is a great inspiration for me. I like to take hikes in the woods. I have a veggie garden, and if the chipmunks don't get to it first, there's food for us. But I don't mind sharing.

www.yaelkrakowski.com

A

A Untitled Pendant, 2010
8.5 x 8.5 x 13 cm
Wool, quartz, glass seed beads, thread; crocheted, stitched
Photo by artist

"Whatever happens in my life is translated into my work."

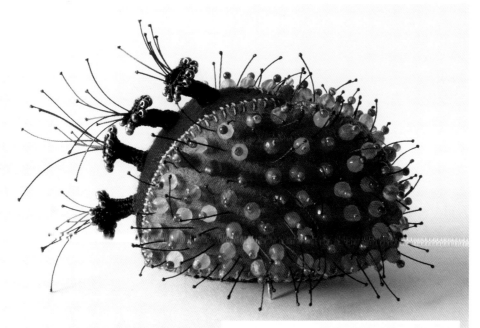

B

B Untitled Brooch, 2010
11.5 x 6.5 x 5.5 cm
Wool, red agate, carnelian, glass seed
beads, thread; stitched
Photos by artist

C Untitled Pendant, 2010
7 x 7 x 10.5 cm
Wool, jade, glass beads, thread; sewn
Photo by artist

C

WHO INTRODUCED YOU TO BEADS?

I discovered beading on my own. I love color and texture, so beads were an easy pick.

WHEN AND HOW DID YOU BEGIN?

In 2001, I moved onto a sailboat in order to sail the Mediterranean Sea, and I wanted to bring work along. I'd done some beading before, but the techniques I developed during that trip marked the start of a beautiful relationship with beads.

HOW DO YOU CHOOSE BEADS?

I choose according to color and texture. The beads have to go along with the mood of the work.

HOW WOULD YOU DESCRIBE YOUR WORK?

My forms are organic. They are nature-, texture-, and color-oriented. The pieces must be wearable!

HOW DO YOU BEGIN A PIECE?

I usually have an idea that I translate into an image. Then I start working with the material that I feel is right. If I do sketches, they're very basic. The rest of the piece develops as I work with the materials.

A

B

134

C

A *Elephantleg Necklace*, 2003
18 cm in diameter
Glass seed beads, cotton
thread; crocheted
Photo by artist

B *Cactus Flower Necklace*, 2008
20 cm in diameter
Oxidized silver, new jade,
yellow turquoise, thread; hand
fabricated, crochet
Photo by artist

C *Flower Ring*, 2006
7.5 x 5 cm
Silver, glass seed beads, cotton
thread; hand fabricated, crocheted
Photos by artist

A

B

A *Berry Necklace*, 2001
5 x 25 cm
Glass seed beads, thread;
crocheted, strung
Photo by artist

B *Desert Brooch*, 2008
4 cm in diameter
Silver, 14-karat gold, carnelian,
garnet, thread; hand fabricated, crocheted
Photos by artist

C

C *Desert Flower Necklace*, 2008
36 cm long
Oxidized silver, carnelian, thread;
hand fabricated, crocheted
Photo by artist

D *Cactus Pendant*, 2008
Necklace: 35 cm in length
Silver, new jade, thread;
hand fabricated, crocheted
Photo by artist

D

WHAT INSPIRES YOU?
Life! The hike I took
today. The color of the
sky. The caterpillar I
just saw. If I'm upset or
happy. Everything!

**HOW HAS YOUR WORK
EVOLVED OVER TIME?**
In terms of shape and
material, it has become
more intricate. I also find
it to be more personal.

**WHAT'S YOUR
FAVORITE PART OF
WORKING WITH BEADS?**
Assembling a piece and
seeing the progress to-
ward the finished work.

**WHAT DO YOU HEAR
IN RESPONSE TO
YOUR WORK?**
"It's beautiful, but I
can't afford it."

"I love Yael's sense of
color and the playful-
ness of her pieces."
—SUZANNE GOLDEN

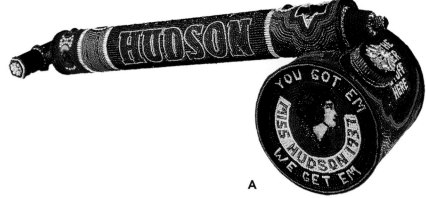

A

We live in Iowa City, Iowa, and have been married for 25 years. A shared interest in Native American beadwork led us to the art we're creating now. This interest was transformed when Tom started beading reproduction Native American objects. Our pieces have been shown internationally and are sold around the United States. We work separately but often consult each other on colors and design. Our pieces aren't planned in advance. The designs develop as row upon row of beads, rhinestone chain, and pins is applied to each object. We hope our work delights viewers and makes them smile.

www.tomandkathywegman.com

tom & kathy wegman

"Beads have the power to transform mundane items into objects of wonder."

B

C

A *Bug Sprayer*, 2011
16 x 12 x 43 cm
Seed beads, rhinestone pins,
adhesive, vintage bug sprayer
Photo by Charlene Trawick

B *Babe Rainbow Skates*, 2010
Each: 23 x 10 x 28 cm
Seed beads, rhinestone chain,
adhesive, vintage roller skates
Photo by Charlene Trawick

C *Beaded Shoes*, 2009
Each: 15 x 8 x 18 cm
Seed beads, rhinestone chain,
adhesive, shoes
Photo by Charlene Trawick

D *Fish Scale*, 2005
29 x 23 x 21 cm
Seed beads, plastic fish and pins,
adhesive, vintage scale
Photo by Charlene Trawick

D

WHAT LED TO YOUR PARTICULAR STYLE AND METHOD OF WORK?
In 1992, Tom saw a beaded taxidermy deer-head form in a book on contemporary beadwork. This inspired him to start beading skulls. The deer head in the book had row after row of beads, and Tom did the same with his skulls. Kathy brought him a vintage camera to bead, followed by a pair of roller skates. Kathy started beading in 1997, after helping Tom fill in areas on a full-size beaded chair. We've used different kinds of beads over the years, although now mostly Japanese seed beads appear in the work because their colors are more intense and there's a greater variety of them.

HOW WOULD YOU DESCRIBE YOUR WORK?
Our work is joyful. People of all ages seem to smile when they see it.

WHAT INSPIRES IT?
Sometimes the shape of an object inspires us. The challenge to transform an object into

something completely different is very inspiring. It's not difficult to work for long hours at a stretch because the work becomes like a meditation. We love to work with color.

TELL US ABOUT YOUR PROCESS AND THE BEADS YOU USE IN THE WORK.

The process has remained the same, but our beads have changed. At first, we only had access to Czech beads. We've always preferred the silver-lined beads because of their shine. Since we discovered Japanese beads, we use them almost exclusively. The only Czech beads that we use now are three-cuts. We string the loose Japanese beads and have all the colors ready. After deciding what to bead, we glue down the first row, then apply row after row. We also use rhinestone pins, vintage glass, and glass beads. We glue beads around the pins. This varies the shape of the rows and adds a new focal point to the work.

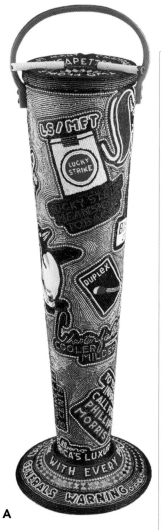

A

B

C   D

A *Floor Ashtray*, 2004
64 x 20 x 20 cm
Seed beads, rhinestone chain,
adhesive, vintage ashtray
Photos by Charlene Trawick

B *Beaded Toaster*, 2004
23 x 13 x 29 cm
Seed beads, adhesive, vintage
toaster, plywood
Photo by Charlene Trawick

C *Can You Spin This Top?*, 2005
20 x 15 x 15 cm
Seed beads, adhesive, toy top
Photo by Charlene Trawick

D *Waffle Iron*, 2010
35 x 26 x 23 cm
Seed beads, glass tiles, rhinestone
pins and chains, adhesive, vintage
waffle iron
Photo by Charlene Trawick

E *Vintage Fan*, 2006
40 x 30 x 18 cm
Seed beads, rhinestone chain and
pins, adhesive, vintage fan
Photo by Charlene Trawick

E

**WHAT'S YOUR
FAVORITE PART OF
WORKING WITH BEADS?**
We love what beads
allow us to accomplish.
We love the color and
the shine.

**WHAT RESPONSES
DO YOU GET TO
YOUR WORK?**
We've never had a
negative response to
our pieces, but maybe
to our prices. Everyone
smiles and wants to
touch the work, which
we allow.

"Tom and Kathy take
ordinary objects and
transform them into
extraordinary objects!"
—SUZANNE GOLDEN

I was born in South Korea and came to the United States to enter the Pratt Institute. I graduated from the school in 2011 with a BFA in jewelry design. While at Pratt, I received the 2011 Myron Toback Award at the Senior Thesis Show. For a period, I worked as a jewelry designer at Miriam Haskell. I now live in Japan.

DESCRIBE YOUR JEWELRY.
I create abstract, organic forms of sea creatures, characterized by tiny, delicate, repeated elements composed of various wires and beads. When my pieces are gathered together, they recreate the atmosphere that exists under the sea.

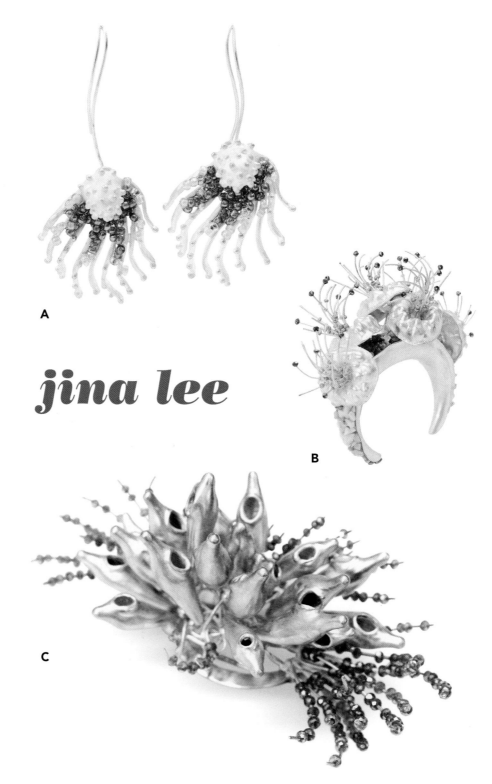

A

jina lee

B

C

"Beads allow me to reinterpret the intriguing colors of the magical world that exists beneath the sea."

A *Spider Flora Earrings*, 2011
Each: 6 x 2.5 x 1.5 cm
Sterling silver, glass beads
Photo by Seung Hun Cha

B *Flora with Coral/Cuff*, 2011
11 x 10 x 6 cm
Sterling silver, coral, crystals
Photo by Seung Hun Cha

C *Huddled Submarine Organism/Brooch*, 2011
7 x 12 x 7 cm
Sterling silver, crystals
Photo by artist

D *Spider Flora Brooch*, 2011
11.5 x 7 x 3.5 cm
Sterling silver, glass beads
Photo by Seung Hun Cha

E & F *Sparkling Flora Ring Set*, 2011
Each: 9 x 9 x 3.5 cm
Sterling silver, crystals
Photos by Seung Hun Cha

WHAT INSPIRES YOU?

I've always had a passionate interest in nature and been captivated by the existence of mysterious organisms in the sea. When I was a child, I was afraid of the sea. It was huge, dark, and deep, and I was afraid it might swallow me. However, the environment under the sea was much more beautiful and exciting than I expected. Oceans are another world that we can't see.

IS THERE MUCH PLANNING AHEAD OF TIME?

I design as I make. I draw a sketch whenever an idea hits me, and then I organize the designs, techniques, and materials. Most of my designs are organic forms, so I usually carve them in wax and cast them. I design the metal pieces first, then choose beads to add variety and color.

"For jewelry, I think Jina's work is outside the box. It's unexpected and unusual wearable art."

—SUZANNE GOLDEN

annette tacconelli

I'm interested in articulating the invisible. I was born a seer with second sight and have given more than 10,000 readings to all kinds of people, from rock stars to janitors. This spiritual component strongly influences my creative process, and most of my art begins from visions that I experience. In college, I studied political thought. After reading Nietzsche's *Beyond Good and Evil*, I acted on my conviction that the courageous life is the artist's. I studied sculpture and performance art at the Art Institute of Chicago and perfected my installation art while working in an avant-garde grocery store. My work has been curated into many national and international exhibits. I now live in the "Holy Land" of Brooklyn, New York, with my husband and son.

www.redlotus108.com

A

A *Moving Still*, 2009
11.4 x 15.2 x 7.6 cm
Found metal, seed beads,
thread; sculptural peyote stitch
Photo by D. James Dee

B *Firewater*, 2007
12.7 x 24.1 x 1.3 cm
Found metal, seed beads,
thread; beadweaving
Photo by D. James Dee

C *Silver*, 2011
5.1 x 7.6 x 7.6 cm
Found metal, silver beads,
cotton, thread; clustered fringe
Photo by D. James Dee

B

C

"Using found, rusted metal is important to me because it allows me to reclaim the discarded moment while emphasizing the aesthetic of imperfect beauty."

My art practice has always included what I call "harvesting"—utilizing what's available and plentiful in my daily life. Found materials feel right and useful. The metals are rich with the time and effort it took to originally create them. I see beauty in the rust, paint, and marks of the world that the metals bear.

HOW DO YOU DESCRIBE YOUR WORK?
Intimate mixed-media sculpture. Sculptural peyote growing off of rusted, found metal.

WHAT INSPIRES IT?
Aesthetically, I'm deeply inspired by the ancient Japanese notions of imperfect beauty. I happily subscribe to the Navajo weavers' belief of a pathway that allows the spirit of the work to flow in and out. The "primitive" goddess religions and their use of small personal totems, fetishes, and sacred objects also inspire me.

AND WHY DO YOU ADD BEADS? HOW DID THAT HAPPEN?
An ordinary, once-discarded piece of metal that I'd had for years changed for me one night. In my mind's

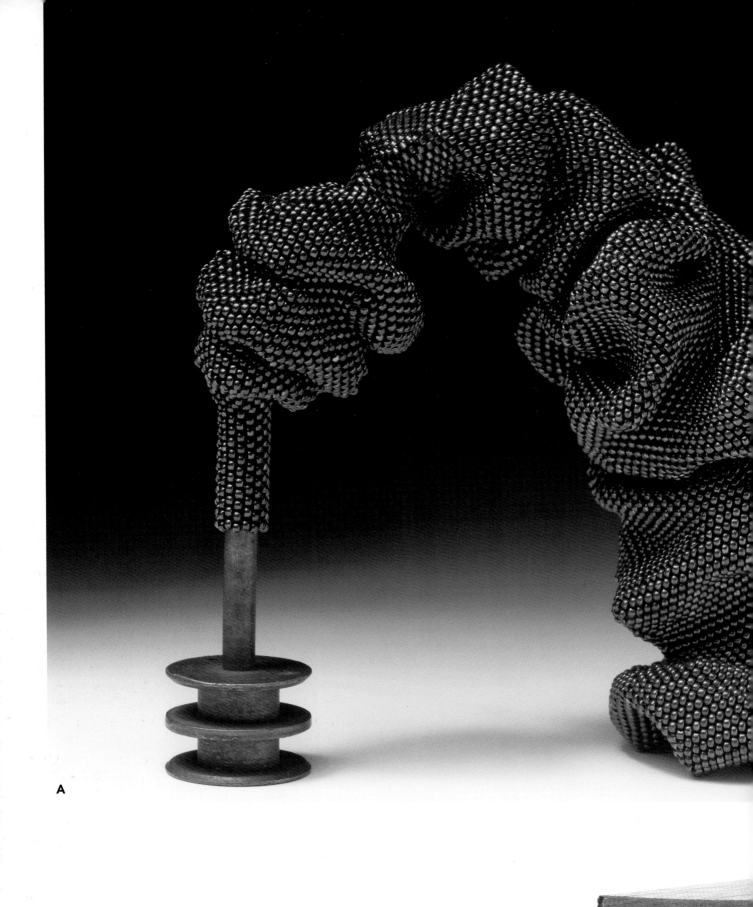

A

B

eye I saw beads on it—
as if invisibly suspended.
I fulfilled this vision
and the sculptures that
came afterward through
a meditative process of
combining beadweaving
or beaded plumes of puff
with post-industrial junk.
These are my Urban Ar-
tIfacts, demonstrations
of the beautiful poten-
tial of the ordinary. The
delicate refinement of
seed beads juxtaposed
against fragments of old
bridges and rusty fences
compels me.

**WHAT'S YOUR
FAVORITE PART OF
WORKING WITH BEADS?**
I love that beads are an-
cient, that cultures from
the primordial to the
present have used them
to embellish their cer-
emonial tools and sacred
totems. And I like the
fact that humble little
seed beads stacked one
over the other in unity
and grace can be viewed
as a metaphor for life,
for the way in which,
moment by moment, we
create our own lives.

**DESCRIBE YOUR
WORKING PROCESS.**
My art is born out of the
metal. I harvest metal
when I see it, from un-
der the Brooklyn-Queens
Expressway, from a
parking lot in DUMBO.

A *Ruffle Eating*, 2009
11.4 x 12.7 x 7.6 cm
Found metal, seed beads,
thread; sculptural peyote stitch
Photo by D. James Dee

B *Bridge*, 2010
5.1 x 52.1 x 8.9 cm
Found metal, seed beads,
thread; beadweaving
Photo by D. James Dee

A

B

A *Undulation*, 2007
12.7 x 17.8 x 3.8 cm
Found metal, seed beads,
thread; beadweaving
Photo by D. James Dee

B *Mandala*, 2009
6.4 x 12.7 x 12.7 cm
Found metal, seed beads,
reclaimed fur, thread, cotton;
peyote stitch, clustered fringe
Photo by D. James Dee

C *Forged*, 2008
10.2 x 30.5 x 35.6 cm
Found metal, seed beads,
thread; beadweaving
Photo by D. James Dee

D *Promising*, 2006
7.6 x 10.2 x 10.2 cm
Found painted metal, seed
beads, thread, cotton;
clustered fringe
Photo by D. James Dee

C

D

I lug it back to my studio and clean it. I put an intriguing piece of it in the center of my worktable and look at it and listen until I receive a vision of the completed piece. I do a quick, gestural sketch. I create samples, because it often takes a few attempts to get the right color, patterning, and effect. Then I begin the actual beading, which can take as many as seventy-five hours and involve upward of 10,000 seed beads.

HOW DO YOU CHOOSE THE BEADS YOU USE?
The colors on the metal I use often dictate the color palette of my chosen beads. Inevitably, I bead and re-bead my pieces, testing color choices and size combinations several times until I achieve a sense of balance within the sculpture.

WHAT RESPONSES DOES THE WORK GET?
Most people automatically try to touch the pieces. Others are curious about the total number of beads used and where the pieces of metal were found.

"Who would have thought of juxtaposing rough, heavy pieces of rusted steel with delicate, refined beads? Brilliant!"

—SUZANNE GOLDEN

jeanette ahlgren

"I believe that whatever medium helps you communicate is the one that you should work with."

I was born in Palo Alto, California, in 1950 and attended Art Center College of Design from 1971 to 1973. The works published here are from 2007 to 2012, during which time I was also caregiver to my mother, who was battling Lewy body dementia. Her incredible spiritual strength and wonderful sense of humor were, and are, my inspiration for both these wire woven structures and structures currently in progress.

A

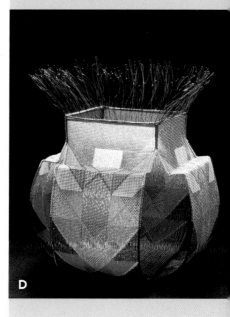

TELL US ABOUT YOUR WORK.

I typically describe my pieces as four-sided, wire-loomed, seed-bead structures.

WHY DID YOU CHOOSE THE FOUR-SIDED VESSEL AS YOUR PRIMARY FORM?

A four-sided vessel with attachment points at the top and base allows for dialogue between the sides but not to such an extent that the viewer is excluded.

AND WHY BEADS?

I didn't really choose beading as my main medium. I was a fiber artist before, and before that I did mixed media, and before that illustration. And before all of that was the Art Center College of Design of Los Angeles, where I was trained in all mediums and then encouraged to experiment with new materials. For some weird reason I'm drawn to modular design, and beads serve me well as a medium.

B

A *#136 Satori*, 2011
46 x 31 x 31 cm
Seed beads; wire woven
Photo by artist

B *#133 Ethos Amped*, 2010
47 x 31 x 31 cm
Seed beads; wire woven
Photo by artist

C *#123 Infinite Spacer*, 2008
48 x 31 x 31 cm
Seed beads; wire woven
Photo by artist

D *#129 Hopes and Fears*, 2010
31 x 31 x 31 cm
Seed beads; wire woven
Photo by artist

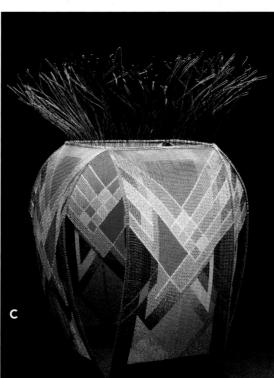

C

WHEN DID YOU BEGIN WORKING WITH BEADS?
I started in 1977 after shipping a group of paintings to a gallery in Hawaii. The construction of a crate for the paintings, the packing, and the sizable air-freight bill that resulted from shipping the work all had a lot to do with the need I felt to "get small." So I bought some rather poor-quality but interesting seed beads, extended the sides of an old pot holder loom, and started weaving. I liked the process. I then invested in some Czech beads and loomed up a couple of necklaces for myself. They turned out well, so I sent color images of them to my gallery in Hawaii, just for fun, really. I think they ordered six with a prepayment contract. Consequently, I quit the job I had at Atari and became a "bead slinger."

HOW DO YOU CHOOSE THE BEADS YOU USE?
I get lucky.

WHAT LED TO YOUR PARTICULAR STYLE AND METHOD OF WORK?
The wire-woven series was inspired by the fuel distributor of a 1980 Porsche 931S.

DESCRIBE YOUR WORKING PROCESS.
My ruffs, or roughs, are etched in stone and sealed in blood.

152

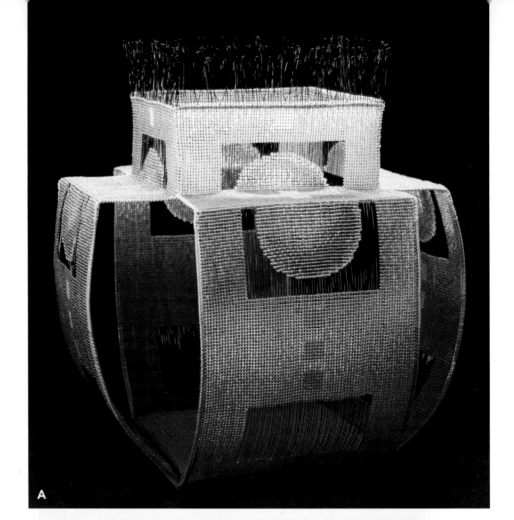

A

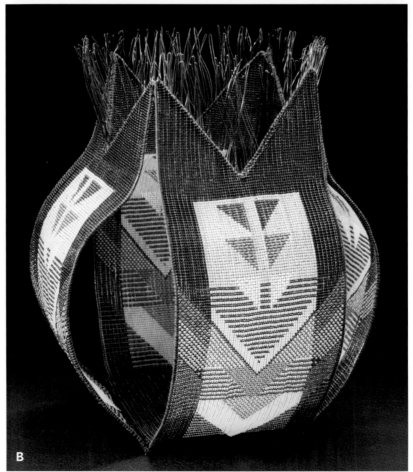

B

Each of my wire-woven structures takes between one and three months to complete. A lot of life can happen in that time, so it's important for me to know where I'm going in my work. This turns the work into something of a sanctuary. It becomes meditative. The fewer surprises or freak-out sessions that I have while I'm looming, the better. Getting the ruff correct is very important, because it saves time. Ripping something out on four sides because the piece "isn't working" is just not something that I care to do. If I get an idea halfway through a piece, I'll draw it and maybe use it for my next structure.

WHAT'S YOUR FAVORITE PART OF WORKING WITH BEADS?

When the fourth side of a piece is finished.

A *#125 Caged Spheres*, 2009
29 x 27 x 27 cm
Seed beads; wire woven
Photo by artist

B *#132 Vivaldi*, 2010
34 x 28 x 28 cm
Seed beads; wire woven
Photo by artist

C *#130 Morning Flight*, 2010
33 x 27 x 27 cm
Seed beads; wire woven
Photo by artist

D *#131 Flow*, 2010
42 x 33 x 33 cm
Seed beads; wire woven
Photo by artist

E *#121 Trust*, 2010
34 x 28 x 28 cm
Seed beads; wire woven
Photo by artist

"Jeanette is truly a master in the art of using color. Adding wire in her looming allows the light to show off her color spectrum."

—SUZANNE GOLDEN

isabell schaupp

I was born in 1969 in Augsburg, Germany, and still call the city home. I'm a trained carpenter and former nurse. In my younger days, I spent several years traveling and learning about life. A graduate of the University of Applied Sciences and Arts in Hildesheim, Germany, where I specialized in metal design, I've participated in numerous national and international exhibitions.

www.isabell-schaupp.de

A

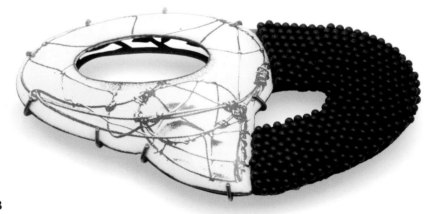

B

"I view my pieces as small catalysts that are attempting to establish contact with their environment."

A *Satellite Shadow No. 5
(Brooch)*, 2011
10.5 x 7 x 0.8 cm
Onyx beads, sterling silver,
copper, enamel, photo,
textile; soldered, sewn
Photo by artist

B *Satellite Shadow No. 8
(Brooch)*, 2011
9.8 x 5.3 x 0.9 cm
Onyx beads, sterling silver,
copper, enamel, photo,
textile; soldered, sewn
Photo by artist

C *Black Ear with Funnel
(Brooch)*, 2011
8 x 6.3 x 2.5 cm
Spinel beads, sterling silver,
copper, enamel, photo,
textile; soldered, sewn
Photo by artist

D *Four Ears (Brooch)*,
2010
7.6 x 8.5 x 2.3 cm
Coral beads, sterling silver,
copper, enamel, photo,
textile; soldered,
crocheted, sewn
Photo by artist

C

D

**YOU USE OTHER
MATERIALS AS WELL
AS BEADS. WHAT ROLE
DO BEADS PLAY IN
YOUR WORK?**
Bead clusters and enam-
eled parts have been
the main ingredients of
my jewelry for the past
three years. The bead
clusters stand side by
side and communicate
with each other, while
the enameled parts,
with their smooth, cold
surfaces, allow me to
"draw" on them with
photographs. The bead
parts have a special
haptic quality. I'm not
all that interested in the
diversity of colors that
beads offer—my own
repertoire is usually
limited to black, red,
and white—but I appre-
ciate the calm graphical
qualities of beads when
they're used in mono-
chrome clusters. They
appear to be three-
dimensional dots.

**HOW WOULD YOU
DESCRIBE YOUR WORK?**
I think my pieces have
a sort of austere beauty
because of the absence
of color. My work isn't
"cute," but it has a poet-
ic quality. Though I use
mainly traditional tech-
niques and materials,
new forms do develop—
forms that often evoke
associations of unknown
flora and fauna.

DESCRIBE YOUR WORK-ING PROCESS. IS THERE MUCH PLANNING INVOLVED, OR DO YOU DESIGN AS YOU MAKE?

Before I start working, I usually have a major topic in mind. It might be a theme like rela-tionships, or it might be an image. My jewelry pieces become inhab-itants of these ideas. Sometimes I have a very clear image of a new piece in mind, but I often develop it through drawing and planning.

WHAT'S YOUR FAVORITE PART OF WORKING WITH BEADS?

I appreciate that bead-ing forces me to be patient. And I enjoy seeing the empty space being filled with beads. It's almost like watching a plant grow.

HOW DID YOU BEGIN USING BEADS?

In 1996, I took a gold-smithing course in Taxco de Alarcón, Mexico. I shared a flat there with a Canadian girl who introduced me to traditional beading. I got a big stock of glass beads in Mexico City and made necklaces, bracelets, and ankle chains for a while. In 2003, I started studying

A

B

A *Necklace with Big Funnel,* 2009
22 cm long
Onyx/white agate beads, sterling silver, enamel, photo, textile; soldered, sewn
Photo by artist

B *Satellite Shadow No. 14 (Brooch),* 2011
9.2 x 6 x 0.9 cm
Onyx beads, sterling silver, copper, enamel, photo, textile; soldered, sewn
Photo by artist

C *Amulet Pouch,* 2010
Pendant: 8 x 19 x 1.6 cm
Onyx/spinel beads, sterling silver, copper, enamel, photo, textile, steel; soldered, sewn
Photo by artist

D *Kobold (Brooch),* 2009
8 x 6.5 x 2.2 cm
Coral beads, sterling silver, copper, enamel, photo, textile; soldered, sewn
Photo by artist

E *Two-Ear Flower (Brooch),* 2009
8.5 x 6.2 x 2.1 cm
Coral beads, sterling silver, copper, enamel, photo, textile; soldered, sewn, crocheted
Photo by artist

C

D

E

jewelry at the University of Applied Sciences and Arts in Hildesheim, Germany. I graduated in 2007. Beads didn't play a major role in my work until about two years ago.

HOW DO YOU CHOOSE BEADS?

The first criterion of choosing beads is color. Other decisive factors include size, structure, and luster. I hardly use glass beads anymore. I prefer working with stone beads like onyx or spinel. My current favorites are small (2 mm) round onyx beads with a matte finish. They're ideal for making clusters and give the surface of a piece a very calm appearance.

"Isabell's pieces of art are meant to be both admired and worn. This is not your grandmother's jewelry!"
—SUZANNE GOLDEN

nick cave

I've been making Sound-suits for almost 20 years. A Missouri native, I hold a BFA from the Kansas City Art Institute and an MFA from the Cranbrook Academy of Art. My work has been exhibited around the world and is included in the public collections of the Museum of Modern Art in New York, the Museum of Contemporary Art in Chicago, and the Smithsonian Institution. My interest in outreach has resulted in perfor-mance projects, residen-cies, lectures, and teach-ing engagements, with invitations from Fabrica, the Benetton Group, and the Smithsonian National Museum. Based in Chi-cago, I'm on the faculty of the School of the Art In-stitute of Chicago, where I serve as chairman of the fashion department and director of the graduate program in Fashion, Body, and Garment.

www.soundsuitshop.com

"I love the way in which beads can change the value of an object, transforming it from the ordinary to the extraordinary."

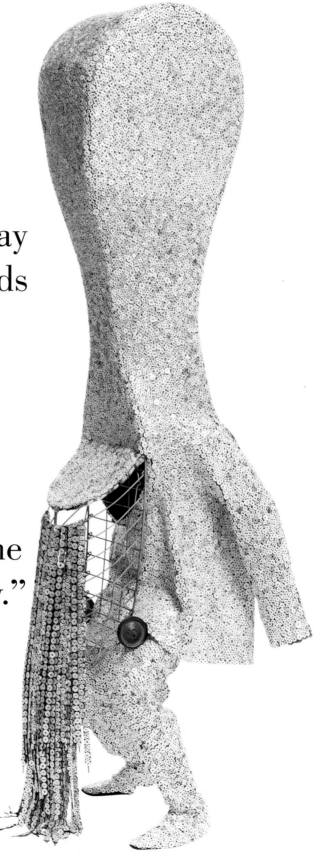

A

B

A Untitled Soundsuit, 2011
248.9 x 96.5 x 83.8 cm
Upholstery, embroidery floss,
mother-of-pearl buttons, shoe-
laces, pushcart, metal armature;
hand sewn
Photo by James Prinz Photography
Courtesy of the artist and the Jack
Shainman Gallery, New York

B Untitled Soundsuit, 2008
248.9 x 96.5 x 83.8 cm
Fabric with appliqués of found
sequined material, yarn, metal
armature; hand sewn, bead
crochet, knitted
Photo by James Prinz Photography
Courtesy of the artist and the Jack
Shainman Gallery, New York

C Untitled, 2009
248.9 x 96.5 x 83.8 cm
Found beaded flowers, metal
armature; hand sewn
Photo by James Prinz Photography
Courtesy of the artist and the Jack
Shainman Gallery, New York

C

**HOW WOULD YOU
DESCRIBE YOUR WORK?**
Playful and seductive.
Luscious on the sur-
face, with dark currents
underneath the layers.
My work is about cel-
ebrating difference and
dreaming bigger.

WHAT INSPIRES IT?
I'm inspired by the
everyday. I'm always
looking, eyes wide open,
at the way in which we
live. I'm also very in-
spired by objects. I may
see something at a flea
market and, from seeing
just that one particular
object, get the inspira-
tion to create an entire
new body of work.

**WHEN AND HOW
DID YOU BEGIN
INCORPORATING BEADS
INTO YOUR WORK?**
I've used beads since I
was young. They were
always around, so I
incorporated them into
garments, objects, etc.

A

A *Speak Louder*, 2011
Each suit: 248.9 x 96.5 x 83.8 cm
Mother-of-pearl buttons, embroidery floss, upholstery, metal armature, mannequin;
hand sewn
Photo by James Prinz Photography
Courtesy of the artist and the Jack Shainman Gallery, New York

B *Untitled*, 2009
248.9 x 96.5 x 83.8 cm
Found beaded funeral wreath, metal armature; hand sewn
Photo by James Prinz Photography
Courtesy of the artist and the Jack Shainman Gallery, New York

C *Untitled Soundsuit*, 2009
248.9 x 96.5 x 83.8 cm
Found abacus, found buttons, embroidery floss, upholstery, metal armature; hand sewn
Photo by James Prinz Photography
Courtesy of the artist and the Jack Shainman Gallery, New York

B

C

HOW DO YOU CHOOSE THE BEADS YOU USE? Whether it's beads on a secondhand garment, found necklaces, or raw bugle beads, I select according to quality, color, pattern, and surplus.

DESCRIBE YOUR WORKING PROCESS. IS THERE MUCH PLANNING INVOLVED, OR DO YOU DESIGN AS YOU MAKE? I design from a place of intuition. I don't sketch, but I do begin with a feeling of the direction I'd like the work to take.

HOW HAS YOUR WORKING PROCESS EVOLVED OVER TIME? With each new work, I ask myself how I can take my art to the next level. How can I exceed expectations, ask more, and dream more? From this, my work continues to evolve, grow, and become even bigger!

A Untitled Soundsuit, 2007
248.9 x 96.5 x 83.8 cm
Appliquéd found beaded and sequined garments, found knit sweaters, metal armature; embroidered, hand sewn
Photo by James Prinz Photography
Courtesy of the artist and the Jack Shainman Gallery, New York

B Untitled Soundsuit, 2009
248.9 x 96.5 x 83.8 cm
Porch screen, found buttons, garment pull-tabs, found hot pads, found knit sweaters; hand sewn
Photo by James Prinz Photography
Courtesy of the artist and the Jack Shainman Gallery, New York

C Untitled Soundsuit, 2005
248.9 x 96.5 x 83.8 cm
Found knit sweaters, embroidery floss, found beaded flowers, metal armature; hand sewn
Photo by James Prinz Photography
Courtesy of the artist and the Jack Shainman Gallery, New York

D Untitled Soundsuit, 2008
248.9 x 96.5 x 83.8 cm
Fabric with appliqués of found
sequined material, yarn, metal
armature; bead crochet, knitted, hand sewn
Photo by James Prinz Photography
Courtesy of the artist and the Jack
Shainman Gallery, New York

E Untitled Soundsuit, 2009
83.8 x 248.9 x 96.5 cm
Found beaded baskets,
vintage papier-mâché rabbit,
appliquéd sequin garments,
metal armature; hand sewn
Photo by James Prinz Photography
Courtesy of the artist and the Jack
Shainman Gallery, New York

E

D

**WHAT RESPONSES
DO YOU GET TO
YOUR WORK?**
My work takes the
viewer to a true place
of purity, where every-
thing feels possible. It
provokes the imagi-
nation and reminds
viewers how important
it is to dream—and to
dream bigger.

"When I see Nick's
work, I'm completely
overwhelmed by the
sheer size of his wear-
able sculptural forms.
His Soundsuits are
made from a wide array
of materials, including
beads, buttons, se-
quins, wire, and other
found objects."
—SUZANNE GOLDEN

about suzanne golden

I'm passionate about creating wearable art. Pictures, paintings, and clothes—all these and more inspire me. If I'm drawn to a concept or an object, whether it's a piece of jewelry, a graphic design, or even just a shape, I try to reinterpret it into a three-dimensional, beaded piece. Beading allows me to combine my ideas with my love of fashion. Color is my biggest influence. I see everything in the world, from people to nature, in terms of color, and this inspires me to create.

Around 1994, I read a newspaper article on bead artist David Chatt. He spoke about glass beads, how light reflects though them and how there was a huge choice of different shades, sizes, and styles for jewelry makers to choose from. He was coming to New York City, where I live, to teach a class, and I immediately signed up. After David's workshop, I was hooked! What appealed to me most about making beaded jewelry was that the colors were already there—and the variety was overwhelming. The number of finishes was also astounding. And I could start designing a piece immediately.

I later discovered the Bead Society of Greater New York and became a member. I took as many classes as possible, wanting to learn everything, and pored over magazines and books. I did Internet research. Through those media, I was able to teach myself beading techniques. I became obsessed and constantly experimented with stitches.

Since those early days, I've become known for several different styles. One of my signature pieces is the black-and-white, tubular-spiral peyote bracelet. This pattern came about because I wasn't content with the basic spiral and started adding graphic patterns. I'm also known for my netted bracelets, which allow me to reveal my color sense.

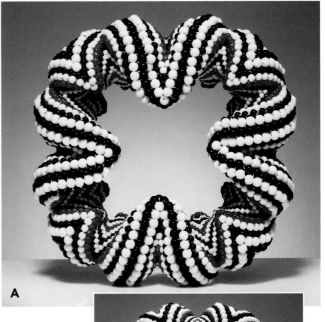

My style has developed over time. I like big, eye-catching, vibrantly hued pieces of jewelry and enjoy incorporating stark graphic patterns. I work on a bold scale; I don't want to waste time creating something small! I get bored easily, so I jump around among various techniques. I always strive for my pieces to make a statement. I try to push the boundaries of beading so that I can express my artistic vision as fully as possible.

www.suzannegolden.com

A *Two Sides Bracelet*, 2012
14 cm in diameter
Acrylic beads, seed beads, braided fishing line; tubular, spiral peyote stitch
Photos by Robert Diamante

B

C

D

E

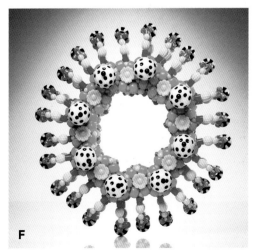

F

B *Square Bracelets,* 2011
Each: 8 x 2.6 cm
Seed beads, acrylic beads; cubic right
angle weave
Photo by Robert Diamante

C *Clown Tie,* 2009
30.5 cm long
Seed beads, crystals, vintage cabachon;
peyote stitch, cross weaving
Photo by artist

D *Desert Bloom Bracelet,* 2010
14 cm in diameter
Acrylic beads, seed beads, wood
beads, rubber beads; cross weaving,
embellished
Photo by Robert Diamante

E *Beaucoup d'Amusement
Necklace,* 2011
66 cm long
Seed beads, acrylic beads; cross
weaving, embellished, stringing
Photo by Robert Diamante

F *Polka Dotty Bracelet,* 2011
16 cm in diameter
Acrylic beads, seed beads;
right angle weave, embellished
Photo by Robert Diamante

A *Ring around the Daisy Bracelet*, 2011
13.5 cm in diameter
Seed beads, acrylic beads;
tubular, spiral peyote stitch
Photo by Robert Diamante

B *Fish in Bloom Bracelet*, 2012
16.5 cm in diameter
Seed beads, acrylic beads, wood
beads; tubular, spiral netting
Photo by Robert Diamante

C *Bracelets*, 2011
Largest: 90 cm in diameter
Seed beads, acrylic beads;
cubic right angle weave
Photo by Robert Diamante

D *Untitled Bracelet*, 2010
16 cm in diameter
Acrylic beads, seed beads, rubber beads; netting, embellished
Photo by Robert Diamante

E *Red Flowers Bracelet*, 2010
15 cm in diameter
Seed beads, acrylic beads;
tubular, spiral peyote stitch
Photo by Robert Diamante

F *Clown Bracelet,* 2009
16 x 9 cm
Seed beads, delicas, crystals,
vintage cabachon; peyote stitch,
cross weaving, embellished
Photo by artist

G *Evolution #5,* 2004
13.9 cm in diameter
Glass seed beads; tubular, spiral peyote stitch
Photo by Robert Diamante

H *Bauble-Licious Necklace,* 2009
33 cm in diameter
Seed beads, acrylic beads;
cross weaving, embellished
Photos by Robert Diamante

I *Plastic Fantastic,* 2011
16.5 cm in diameter
Acrylic beads; tubular, spiral peyote stitch
Photo by Robert Diamante

additional photo credits

Thank you to the photographers who took portraits of the artists featured in this book, in order of appearance:

Christian Kaiser, page 6

Peter Völker, page 10

Dawn Greene, page 14

Edward Wilkinson Latham, page 10

Editions in Craft, page 16

Jan Visser, page 26

Larry Sanders, page 32

Alvar Gullichsen, page 42

Phil Huling, page 52

Eliezer Krakowski, page 124

Dan Kvitka, page 58

Tom Dolack, page 64

Graham Carruthers, page 68

Gail Handelmann, page 74

Matthew F. Napoleon, page 78

Phil Pope, page 82

Laszlo Bodo, page 86

Rens Horn, page 102

Peter Millett, page 112

Hugh Kraemer, page 116

The Iowa City Press-Citizen, page 130

Yun Son Choe, page 134

D. James Dee, page 136

Shannon Wall, page 142

James Prinz Photography, page 150

The photos of Suzanne Golden, Estyn Hulbert, Eva Maria Keiser, Sari Liimatta, Colleen O'Rourke, Christy Puetz, Isabell Schaupp, and Uliana Volkhovskaya are all self-portraits.

acknowledgments

I want to personally thank the contributing artists, each and every one, for their invaluable participation. This book is about them, and without all their incredible art, there wouldn't be a book. I would also like to thank my talented editor Nathalie Mornu for her invaluable assistance in all aspects of pulling this volume together.

index